Year 9
GRAPHICS
A course of work by Paul Bourdōt

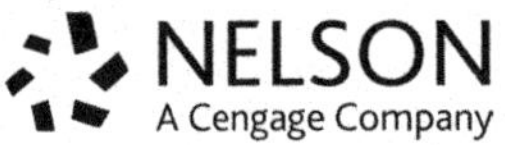

Year 9 Graphics Textbook
1st Edition
Paul Bourdot

Design and Typeset by: Book Design Ltd
Production controller: Siew Han Ong
Reprint: Jess Lovell

Any URLs contained in this publication were checked for currency during the production process. Note, however, that the publisher cannot vouch for the ongoing currency of URLs.

Acknowledgements
Kerry Guy for allowing the use of the examples on page 19 and the British Paints logo on page 21 from his book 'Understanding Technical Drawing Book One'.

Matthew Beneka, Year 9 Long Bay College, for allowing me to use his work as exemplars.

Richard Lee and Ashleigh Lloyd, Year 13 Long Bay College, for lending me their hands for the photographs demonstrating the correct use of instruments.

Printed in Australia by Ligare Pty Limited.
3 4 5 6 7 8 9 21 20 19 18 17

For product information and technology assistance,
in Australia call **1300 790 853**;
in New Zealand call **0800 449 725**

For permission to use material from this text or product, please email
aust.permissions@cengage.com

National Library of New Zealand Cataloguing-in-Publication Data
Year 9 graphics (textbook) : a course of work / by Paul Bourdot.
ISBN 978-017018-561-5
1. Mechanical drawing—Textbooks. 2. Geometrical drawing— Textbooks. [1. Mechanical drawing. 2. Geometrical drawing.]
I. Title.
604.20712—dc 22

Cengage Learning Australia
Level 7, 80 Dorcas Street
South Melbourne, Victoria Australia 3205

Cengage Learning New Zealand
Unit 4B Rosedale Office Park
331 Rosedale Road, Albany, North Shore 0632, NZ

For learning solutions, visit **cengage.co.nz**

CONTENTS

ISBN 978-0170185615

INTRODUCTION

This guide has been written to accompany the *Year 9 Graphics Worksheets*. It has been designed for students to use as a 'how to' resource.

However, this resource is not intended to be given to students without instruction from the teacher. Teachers will need to pre-plan their approach to using the worksheets and this guide, and be proactive in teaching the skills required to successfully complete each exercise.

The exercises will challenge students but at the same time enable them to acquire a range of skills, providing a foundation on which to build in future years. Students who study this course will have a head start in basic drawing systems and will develop a sense of personal satisfaction in the completion of each.

The exercises should not be rushed. Some will take longer to complete than others and can be used as homework exercises, but teachers must monitor student progress and ensure the emphasis is on *quality* rather than *quantity*.

Students must develop an awareness of the need for perseverance, good time management and to strive for accuracy and precision of lines.

The topics and skills covered are essential for NCEA success in senior school.

Although the exercises are for 50 minute lessons, 5 days per week, covering an approximate 19 week course, they may be adapted to suit other course durations.

The exercises are set out in a suggested order of presentation to a class, allowing for the progressive development of skills and understanding.

All exercises have been tested and refined over many years of teaching, and I can attest to the high degree of satisfaction and success that students have gained from them.

Instilling a sense of excitement and pride in the subject, establishing the skills for NCEA success and retaining students with the right skills for their senior years, is essential to the future of Graphics and its status within our schools.

I wish to thank the many students who give me reasons each day to continue teaching.

Paul Bourdōt

Suggested Time Frame

The following weekly time frame **is a suggestion only** and should be modified to suit. Much of the work, once started in class, should be completed as homework where appropriate.

Depending on the ability of the class, some work could be modified or not expected to be attempted by some students.

One unit of work well done with sound understanding is preferable to two or more units rushed and poorly executed.

	The Course	The Skills
1	**Worksheets 1, 2 & 3** Establish class routines and management procedures. Provide students with equipment. WORKSHEETS COMPLETED FOR HOMEWORK.	• Pencil types – 2H, how to hold, use and sharpen. • Reading a ruler and the transfer of measurement from ruler or set square. Use of eraser. • Lines – constructions and outlines. Drawing sequence and simple rendering. • Printing standards.
2	**Worksheet 4** Setting up an A3 page on the drawing board and making a TITLE BLOCK.	• Printing standards – upper case between guide lines. • Correct pencil used – 2H for lines, HB for printing. • Drawing sequence emphasised.
3	**Worksheet 5** Introduction to the COMPASS and drawing circles and curves.	• The compass – sharpening/holding/using. Radius and Diameter explained. Setting of radius from ruler/set square. lines – Centre line. • Correct lead in compass – HB. • Drawing sequence emphasised again.
4	**Worksheet 6** Orthographic Projection.	• Correct pencil – 2H. • Drawing sequence emphasised again. • The importance of projection to obtain views. • LINES – Hidden Detail, Reference Line. • Introduction to the Projection Symbol and the Projection Box. • Neatness, accuracy, page layout.
5	**Worksheet 7** Orthographic Projection.	• Correct pencil – 2H. • Drawing sequence emphasised again. • The importance of projection to obtain views. • LINES – Hidden Detail, Reference Line. • Placing circles in a drawing. • Neatness, accuracy, page layout.
6	**Worksheet 8 – At School** Rendering of solids. **Worksheet 9 – At Home** Collect and paste logo research with design notes.	• 4B pencil rendering to provide tonal values. • Light direction and its importance to creating realism. • Tissue smudging, erasing shield to sharpen edges.
7	**Worksheet 10 – At School** 3D freehand sketching. **Worksheet 9 – At Home** Logo concepts with design notes.	• 4B pencil used. • Importance of straight, parallel lines. • No instrument use. • Crating to obtain proportions. • Colour pencil rendering – tone and materials.

ISBN 978-0170185615

	The Course	The Skills
8	**Worksheet 15 – At School** Oblique Drawing. **Worksheets 11 & 12 – At Home** 2D and 3D rapid viz sketches.	• Oblique drawing introduction – axes, lines, drawing sequences etc. • Sketching introduced at school, completed at home.
9	**Worksheet 16 – At School** Isometric Drawing. **Worksheets 13 & 14 – At Home** 2D detailed and 3D exploded sketches.	• Isometric drawing introduction – axes, lines, drawing sequence etc. • Sketching introduced at school, completed at home.
10	**Worksheet 17 – At School** Isometric circles and curves.	• Instrumental skills and drawing sequence reinforced. • Isometric circles and curves, compass constructions.
11	**Worksheet 18 – At School** Isometric circles and plotting with a compass or dividers. **At Home** Collect research for design assignment.	• Isometric circles. • Plotting from a given view into isometric. • Using the ellipse template.
12	**Design Assignment** Research, concept sketches, design notes relating to specs using design language.	• Begin concept sketches for design assignment, linking to the research collected previously (Complete for homework).
13	**Design Assignment** Design development sketches, design notes relating to specs using design language.	•Begin design development sketches for design assignment, based on the chosen concept (Complete for homework).
14	**Design Assignment** Orthographic Projection.	• Begin an orthographic projection of the chosen concept, drawn to scale (Complete for homework).
15	**Design Assignment** Instrumental pictorial drawing.	• Begin an instrumental pictorial drawing (isometric or oblique) of the chosen concept. Render and make a background (Complete for homework).
16	**Design Assignment – At Home** Evaluation and assembly of all drawings. **Worksheet 19 – At School** One point perspective drawing.	• Discussion of all the specifications. • All pages stapled down left side to be opened like a book. • Introduction to one point perspective drawing skills – circles and equal space division.
17	**Worksheet 20** Two point perspective drawing.	• Introduction to two point perspective drawing skills – equal space division, landscape graphics.
18	**Worksheets 21–25** Any combinations depending on available time.	
19	**Worksheets 21–25** Any combinations depending on available time.	

ISBN 978-0170185615

The Teaching Environment

It is important that the graphics room is set up with the necessary equipment and that it is maintained in good working order. This page shows the equipment that students in my school purchase in the first week of the course. The photos on the next page show how I have set up my classroom.

Student Personal Equipment

All students purchase their own equipment (a graphics kit) and pay a materials fee to cover its cost. Graphics kits are purchased by the department and given to each student in the first week of the course. Each kit contains basic drawing products within the carry bag shown which is stored at school in a designated cupboard. Students are taught to take responsibility for their kit, especially when it is taken home for homework, and to make sure that it is at school for every graphics lesson.

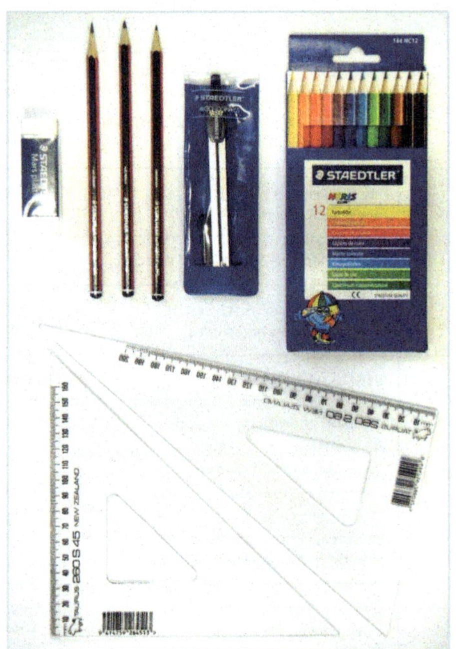

- 1 30/60° set square
- 1 45° set square
- 1 Eraser
- 1 A3 plain drawing block
- 1 2H and HB pencil
- 1 4B pencil
- 1 set of 12 Colouring pencils
- 1 20 sheet A3 drawing block
- 1 Compass
- 1 A3 zip-up carry case

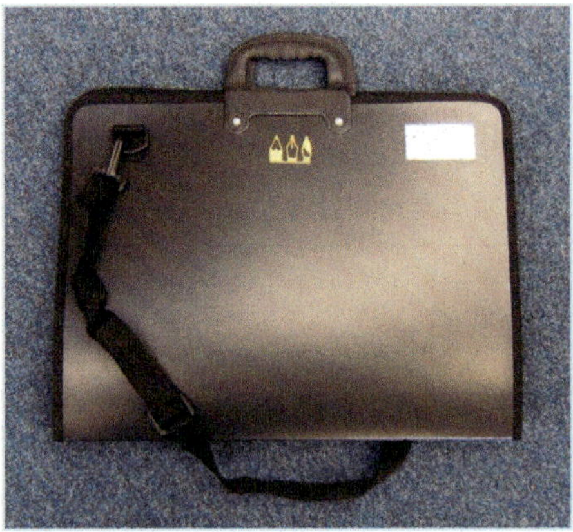

ISBN 978-0170185615

In setting up my classroom, a deliberate attempt has been made to ensure that it works for both teacher and student, so that students enjoy being there and that the necessary equipment is available to do the job.

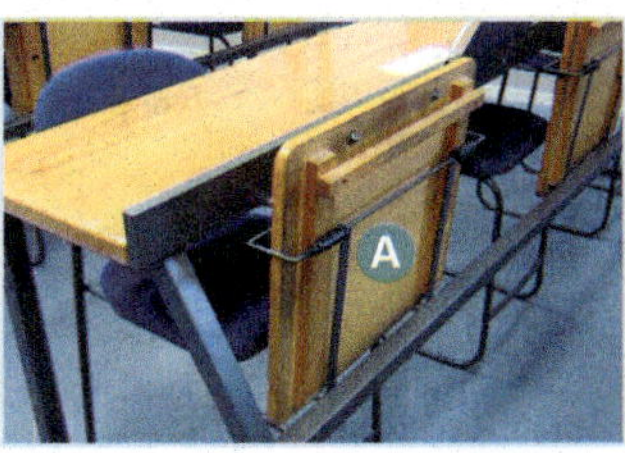

Student workspaces consist of the following:

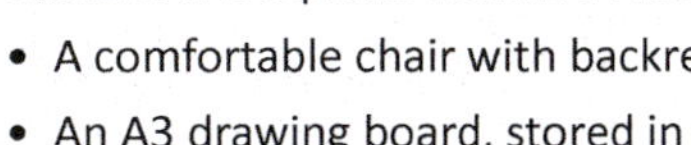

- A comfortable chair with backrest.
- An A3 drawing board, stored in a cradle at the front of the workspace when not in use (**A**). This allows the flat part of the desk to be used for sketching, rendering, and model making etc, preserving the drawing board for instrumental work only. *A groove along the bottom of the board is provided for students to place their pencils.*
- A tee square. When not in use it is stored on a hook at the end of the desk.
- A 'pull out' pencil sharpening drawer (**B**). Consists of a replaceable strip of fine sandpaper, a strip of plain paper, and a pad of carpet. It is used to keep the point of the pencil sharp while working, to ensure line consistency.
- A rack for the placement of worksheets to keep the work surface tidy and to allow room for equipment to be laid out (**C**).
- A quick reference chart, attached to the desk top, that shows line types and printing standards (**D**).
- The drawing board cradle doubles as a place to store the graphics kit when the drawing board is being used (**A**).

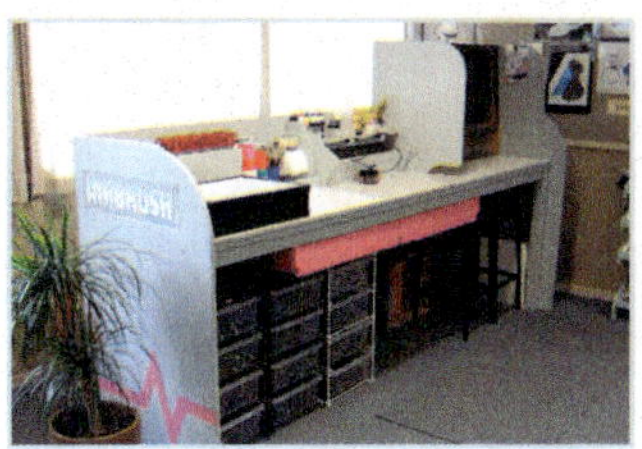

Spare paper, pencils and set squares as well as class sets of scissors, craft knives, markers and an airbrushing workstation that students may access are also provided in the room.

ISBN 978-0170185615

Pencils

H means a hard lead, B means a softer lead. Use three types of pencil:
2H for all lines, **HB** for printing, **4B** for freehand sketching.

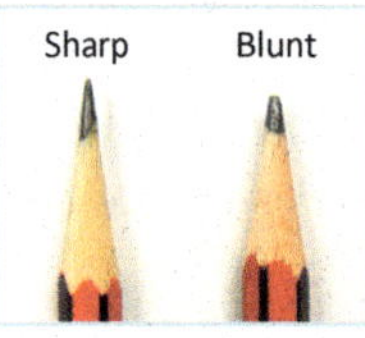

Sharpening

Keep your pencils sharp by using a pencil sharpener. As you work and the end gets rounded, sharpen it on a sharpening block. You can easily make one of thin wood with a strip of fine sandpaper glued to the surface (right).

Thin wood or plastic

Fine sandpaper

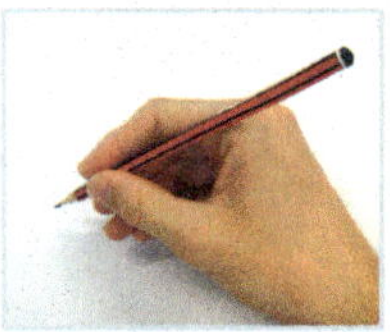

Holding

Hold your pencil so that there is equal pressure between the thumb, the side of the middle finger and the tip of the index finger. Bend your fingers slightly. This is called the tripod grip.

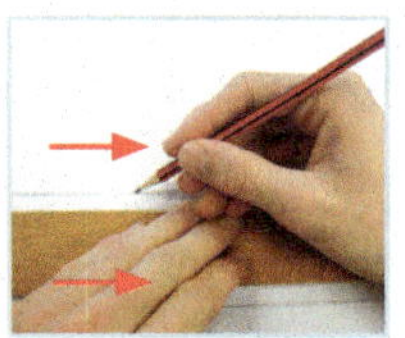

Drawing a Horizontal Line

Hold your tee square with your left hand fingers beneath the line you are drawing, keeping the pressure inwards.

Angle your pencil inwards toward the top of the tee square and **drag your pencil** from left to right to make the line.

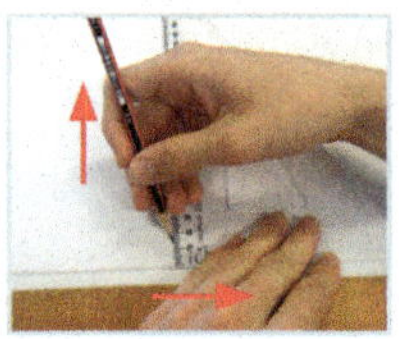

Drawing a Vertical Line

Hold your tee square with the palm of your other hand, fingers also holding the set square in place. Angle your pencil inwards toward the edge of the set square then **drag your pencil upwards** to make the line.

Drawing a Line on an Angle

Hold your tee square with the palm of your left hand, fingers also holding the set square in place. Angle your pencil inwards toward the edge of the set square, then:

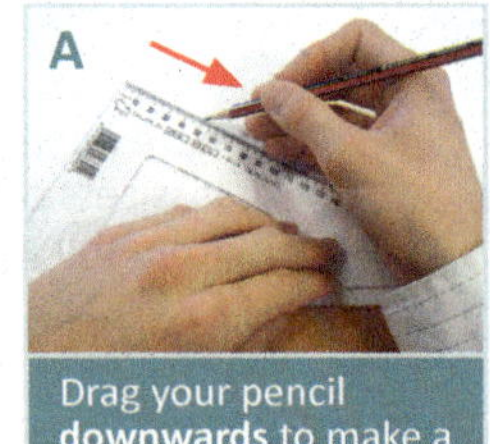

Drag your pencil <u>downwards</u> to make a line that slopes down.

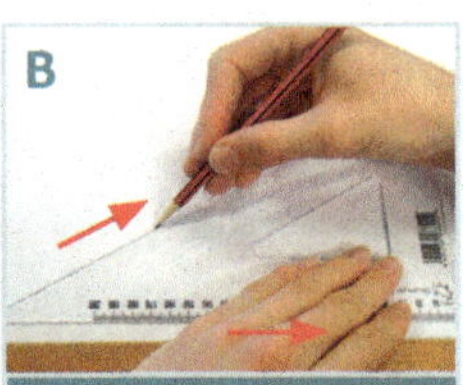

Drag your pencil <u>upwards</u> to make a line that slopes up.

ISBN 978-0170185615

Lines

There are different lines for different purposes. And there are different thicknesses and degrees of darkness of lines.

Construction lines

The first lines of every drawing. They are very light, thin lines and are easily erased.

Outline

The darkest lines. These are thin, dark lines to show outlines and outside edges of objects.

Hidden detail

Medium darkness lines. They are short, thin dashes that show parts that are hidden behind surfaces. They are placed on the drawing after the outlines.

Centre lines

Medium darkness, thin lines. They are a short dash and a long line to show objects/parts that are equal each side of a centre (circles, etc).

Reference lines

Medium darkness, thin lines. They are a long line broken by two short dashes to show the fold lines between planes in an orthographic projection.

On **Worksheet 1 Getting Started**, practice drawing the lines as shown.

Use your 2H pencil to make them construction lines first (very light). Then turn some into outlines (dark and thin) by carefully placing the darker line directly on top of the construction line.

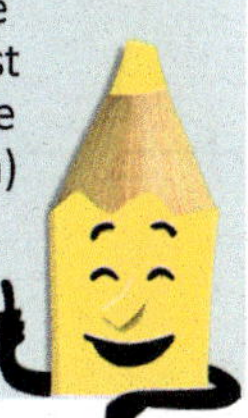

Horizontal

45°

60°

30°

Vertical

Rules

- Drag your pencil, never push it.
- When making outlines (called lining in) **twist your pencil** as you draw to keep the end sharp and the line thin.

ISBN 978-0170185615

Measuring Along Lines

Measuring distances along lines is always done at the construction stage.

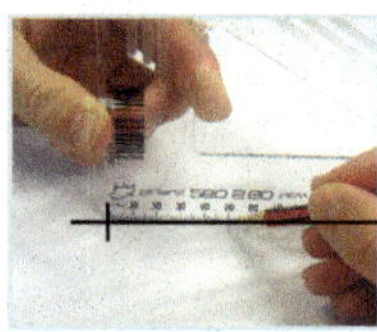

Step 1
Draw the line or lines in very light construction. Make a short line **(a dash, not a dot)** at the beginning of the line, from which to measure.

Step 2
Hold the set square between your finger and thumb as shown. Rest it on its edge on the construction line so that the printed numbers are **facing towards you**.

Line up the first millimetre mark of the set square with the dash at the beginning of the line, then step off the required length with your pencil, making another dashed line, **not a dot**.

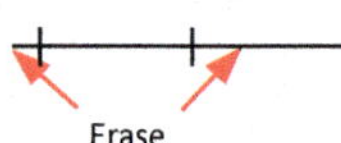

Step 3
Check that the distance is correct then erase the unwanted parts of the line. Check again then carefully outline with a sharp, thin line **directly on top** of the light construction line. Twist the pencil as you draw.

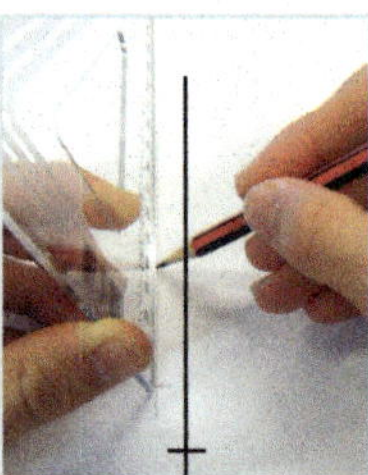

Measuring Vertical Lines

Hold the set square between your finger and thumb as before. Rest it on its edge on the construction line so that the printed numbers can be **viewed from the right**.

Step out the distance as before, making a dashed line, **not a dot**.

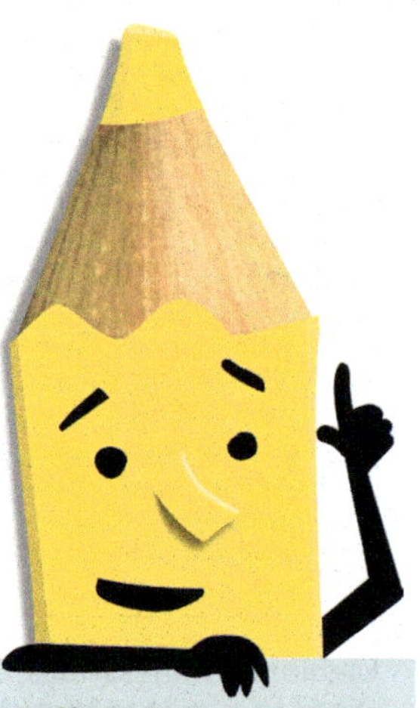

Collect Some Good Habits

Right from the start it is important that you get into the right habits.

Check out the list of things below.

- Wash your hands.
- Always be neat and accurate.
- Use a soft cloth to clean your gear.
- Keep your pencils sharp.
- Look after your equipment and use it only for Graphics.

ISBN 978-0170185615

Measuring Lines and Drawing Sequences

The correct sequence for placing a drawing on the page will save time and help prevent mistakes.

Follow the Steps to Drawing Success

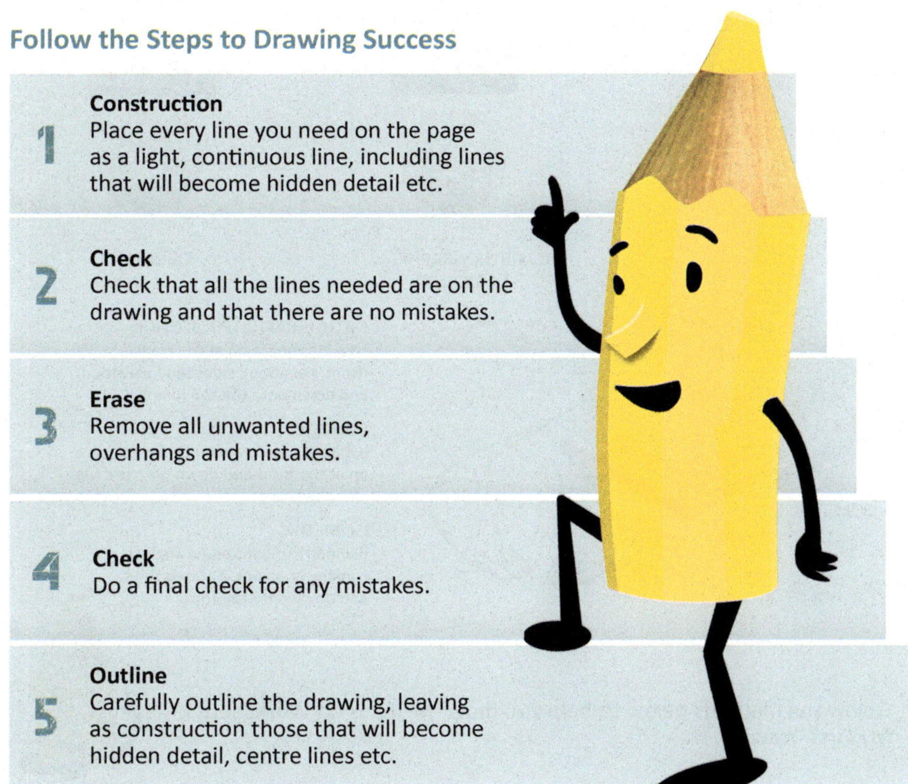

1 **Construction**
Place every line you need on the page as a light, continuous line, including lines that will become hidden detail etc.

2 **Check**
Check that all the lines needed are on the drawing and that there are no mistakes.

3 **Erase**
Remove all unwanted lines, overhangs and mistakes.

4 **Check**
Do a final check for any mistakes.

5 **Outline**
Carefully outline the drawing, leaving as construction those that will become hidden detail, centre lines etc.

Last of All

After the drawing has been outlined, place all other lines that are not outlines such as centre lines, hidden detail and reference lines.

Rule
If it's not an outline, it's not a dark line.

ISBN 978-0170185615

There are three main ways to draw things in Graphics:

ORTHOGRAPHIC PROJECTION

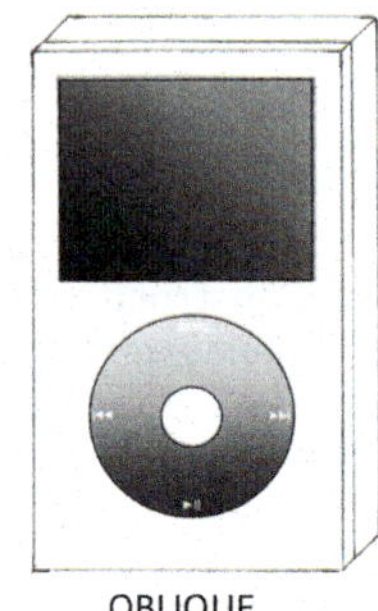

OBLIQUE

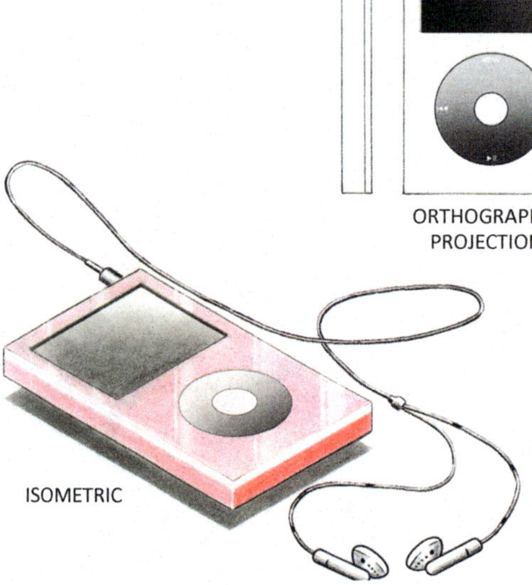

ISOMETRIC

ORTHOGRAPHIC PROJECTION
Looking square on at the front (front elevation), sides (end elevation) and down onto the top (plan).

OBLIQUE
(Oblique means angle) Looking square on at the front and down onto the top and one side.

ISOMETRIC
(Isometric means equal angles) Looking at an angle at two sides and down onto the top.

Follow the methods below to help you draw the iPods on **Worksheet 2 My First Drawing.**

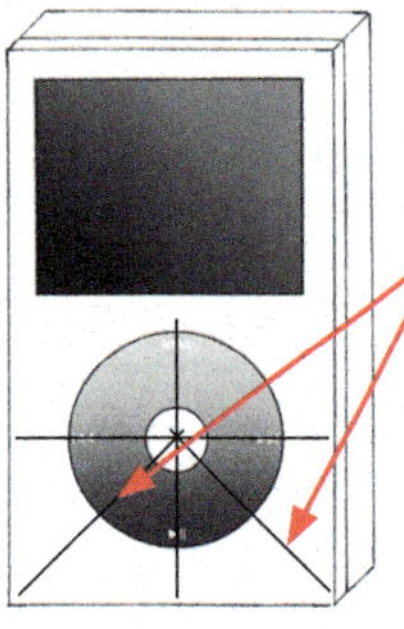

Two equal angles (45°) will locate the centre of the click wheel. Make sure the lines are *very light construction lines*. Use a **circle template** to draw the two circles of the click wheel. Circle templates are available from graphic supply outlets.

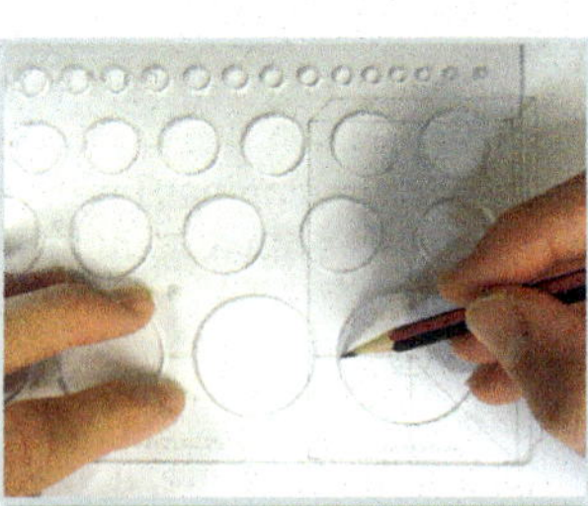

Using a circle template

ISBN 978-0170185615

Finishing Your Drawing

To make the drawing look professional, make the screen and the isometric click wheel (an ellipse) shown below, on a computer. Print them out and paste them onto the drawings.

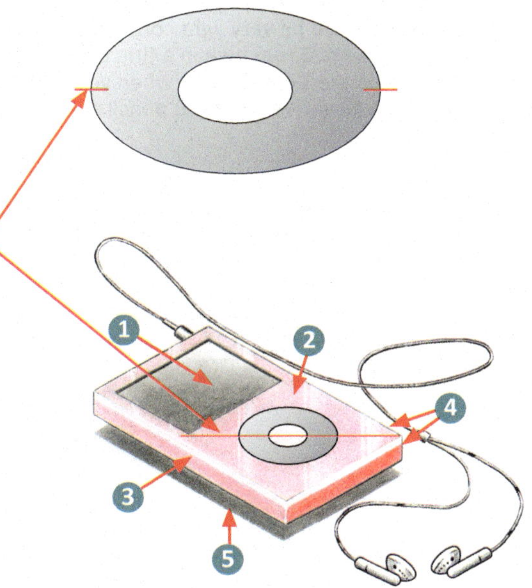

Draw a **horizontal** construction line through the top of the isometric drawing and through the centre of the ellipse before you cut it out.

You can then line the ellipse up to both lines, paste it on and carefully erase the lines.

Take lots of care when pasting. To avoid smears across the drawing use only a small amount of glue.

Note: Paste the click wheel after the drawing has been rendered.

Rendering

Simple rendering has been used to make the isometric drawing look real. The comments below will help you achieve this look. The numbers refer to the rendered drawing above.

1 The screen can be made to look shiny by using a 4B pencil smudged with a tissue *(see page 28)*, leaving a whiter area near the top corner. Edges have been outlined with a sharp HB pencil. Clean up any smudges around the screen with your eraser against a piece of paper *(see page 28)*.

2 Coloured pencil has been used on the body of the iPod: top surface light, left side darker, right side darkest. Shine has been made with vertical eraser stripes against a piece of paper *(see page 28)*. Make a wide stripe with a thin one next to it.

3 The edges of the iPod have been made white with an eraser against a piece of paper to make a thin, white line *(see page 29)*.

4 The outside edges have been darkened with a sharp HB pencil.

5 A shadow has been added for a 3D effect. Draw this with your 30° set square. Smudge 4B pencil with a tissue, then sharpen the edges with an eraser against a piece of paper.

ISBN 978-0170185615

The neatness of your printing on your drawings is very important in Graphics.

Rules

- Upper case (capital) letters are used.
- Printing is always between guide lines to keep the height of the letters the same.
- Guide lines should be very light construction lines drawn with a sharp 2H pencil.
  Guide lines are **5 mm** high in a title block.
  Guide lines are **3–4 mm** high when you add printing around a drawing.
- Printing is done with a sharp HB pencil and made dark enough to be easily read.

ABCDEFGHIJKLMNOPQRSTUVWXYZ

Very light guide lines

0123456789

4 ← This style of 4 can also be used

When there are two or more rows of printing, leave a gap between the rows. Make the gap the same height as the guide lines.

· GRAPHICS IS COOL

· GRAPHICS IS NEAT

· USING A TEE SQUARE IS REALLY SWEET

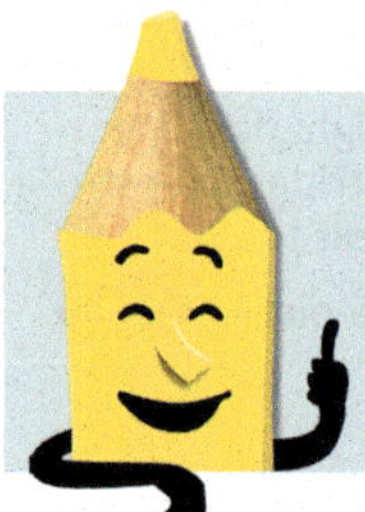

Remember

Never rush your printing. Take your time to form every letter carefully and accurately.

Using the lettering styles above, copy the graphics poem on **Worksheet 3 Printing**.

ISBN 978-0170185615

The Title Block and Printing 3

Most drawings you will draw with your instruments will be on a page that has a TITLE BLOCK. Title blocks can have different designs but are best kept simple.

The title block is placed at the bottom of the paper to show the date the drawing was drawn, the scale if appropriate (how much smaller or larger the drawing is to its full size), the name of the drawing and the name of the person who did the drawing.

A simple title block is shown below. Set it out at the bottom of **Worksheet 4 Beginning Drawing,** to the sizes given, making all lines construction lines to begin with.

The title block has TWO types of lines with two types of pencil used.

Lines

- Construction lines for the printing guide lines *(very light lines).*
- Outlines for all other lines *(dark, thin lines).*

Pencils

- 2H for all lines.
- HB for printing.

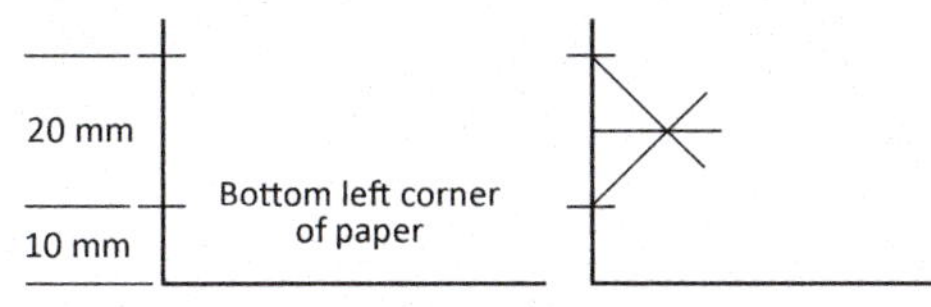

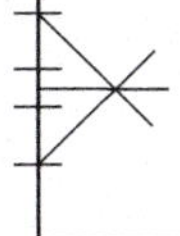

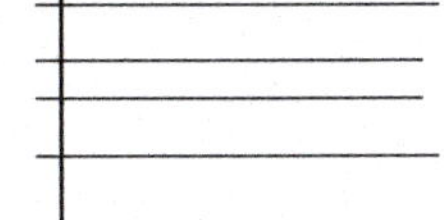

Step 1
Measure the height of the title block.

Step 2
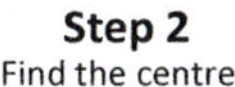
Find the centre.

Step 3
Measure the height of the printing guide lines 2.5 mm each side of the centre (5 mm total).

Step 4
Use your tee square to extend all four lines across the page. Draw the two verticals (120 mm) and outline all lines except the two 5 mm printing guide lines.

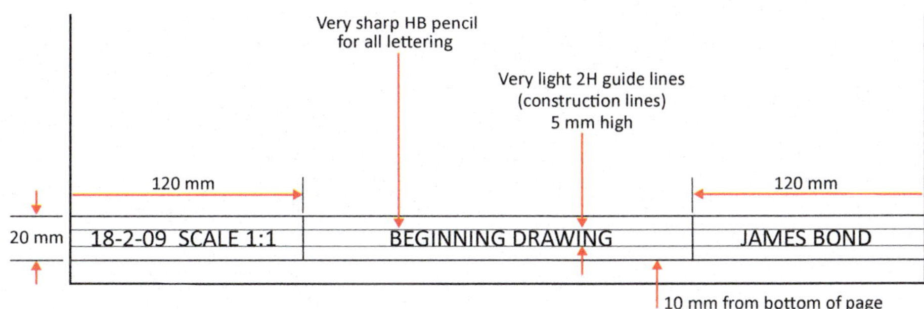

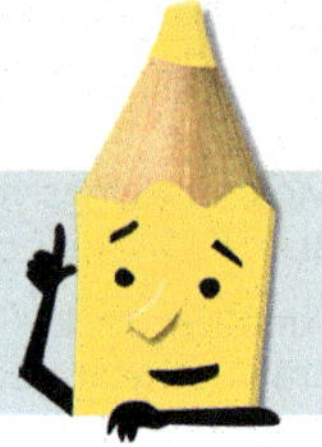

Beginning Drawing

Do the following exercises on **Worksheet 4 Beginning Drawing**, which should have the title block you have just drawn.

1 Two shapes are shown, Exercise 1 and 2, which are based on constructing squares with horizontal and vertical lines, and 45° angles.

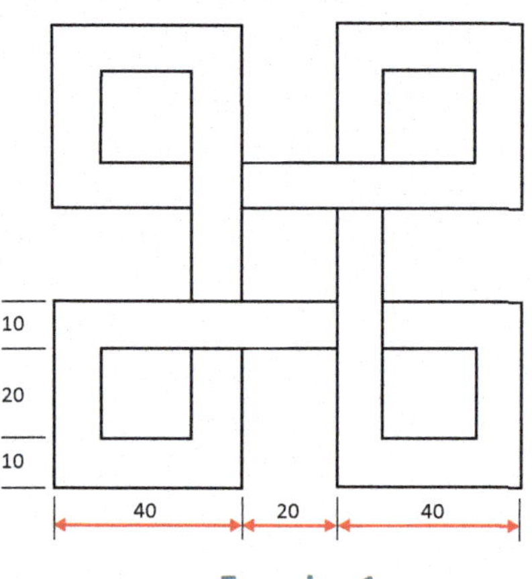

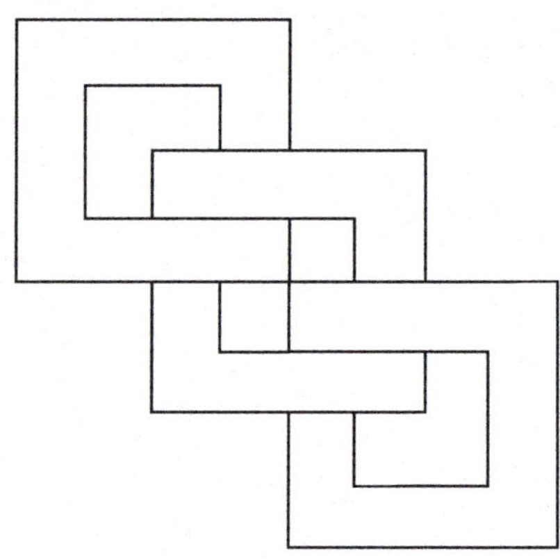

Exercise 1 **Exercise 2**

2 Using your tee square, set squares and a sharp 2H pencil, carefully redraw each, following the steps on the next page and the starting positions shown in the page layout.

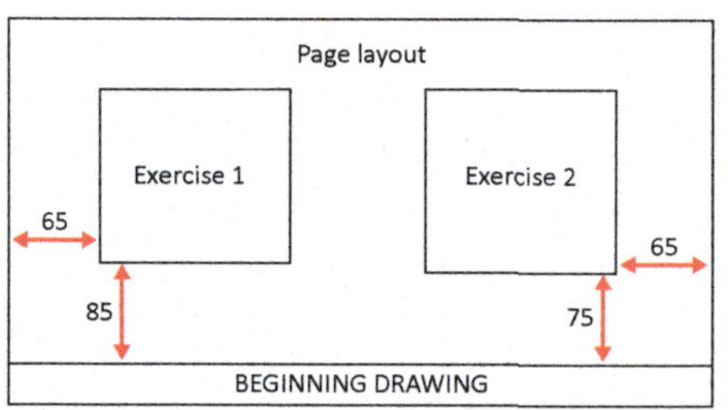

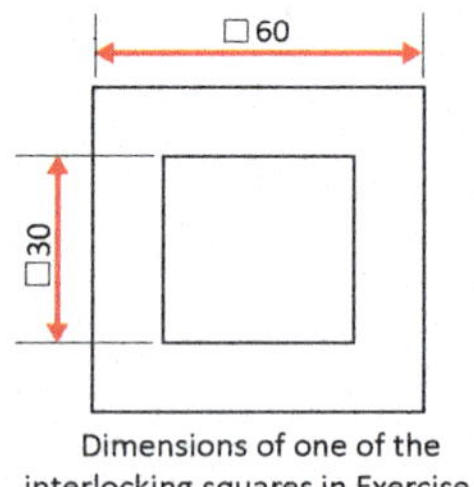

Dimensions of one of the interlocking squares in Exercise 2

ISBN 978-0170185615

Exercise 1: Method

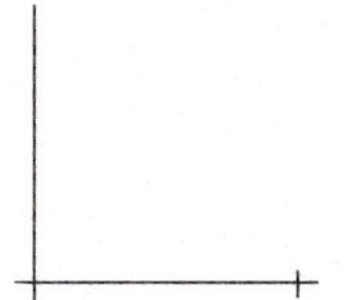

Step 1
Draw a horizontal line and set out its length (100 mm). Draw a vertical line.

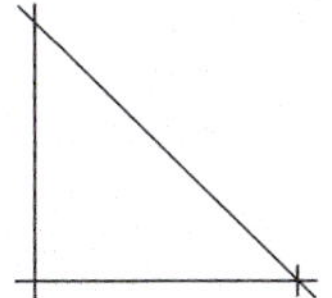

Step 2
Draw a diagonal line (45°) from the bottom right to touch the vertical line.

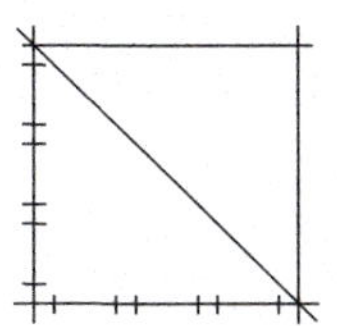

Step 3
Draw the top and right side of the square and set out the sizes of the shape.

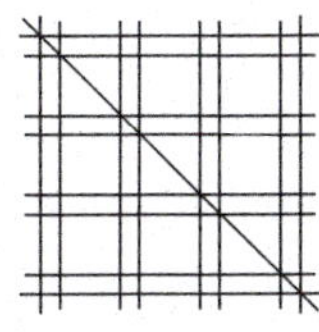

Step 4
Draw a grid, erase unwanted lines, check and outline the shape.

Exercise 2: Method

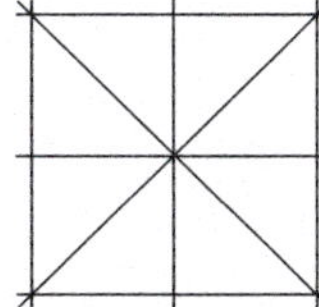

Step 1
Set out a square (120 mm) as in Exercise 1, and divide into four further squares.

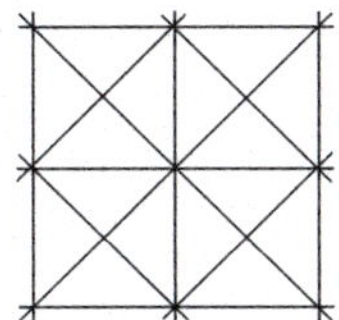

Step 2
Cross the diagonals of each square to find their centres.

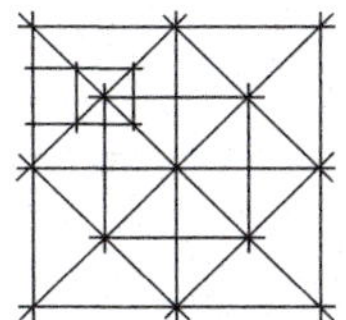

Step 3
Draw the middle square where the diagonals touch, then set out the sizes of the internal square. Extend lines to touch the diagonals.

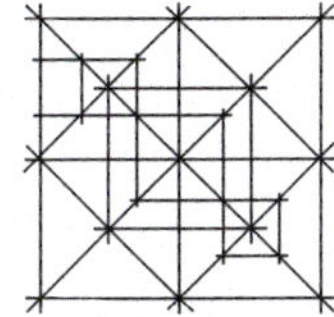

Step 4
Continue extending lines to touch the diagonal of each square to form the three links Erase unwanted lines and outline the shape.

Exercise 3

When finished, here is a further exercise you may like to try on the back of the sheet.

Begin with the horizontal line A, then draw line B. Measure the length of B (80 mm)and draw the vertical line C.

Now draw line D at 90° to B (it will be a 45° line) and measure 20 mm along it to find and draw line E, parallel to line B.

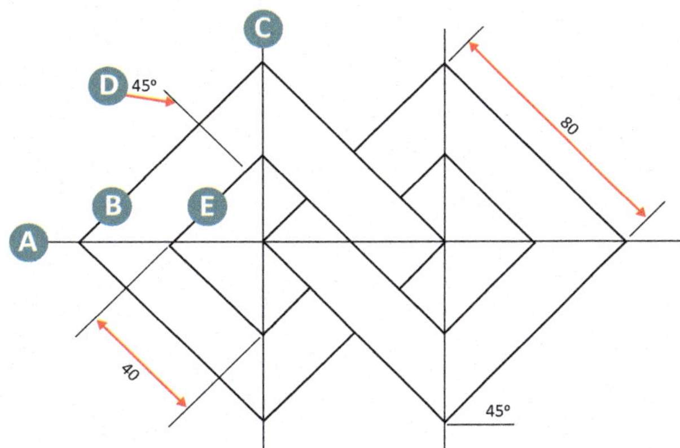

ISBN 978-0170185615

Circles

Here are the names and symbols you need to know about when drawing circles.
Note the broken line (CENTRE LINE) through the middle.

Diameter
Is the distance from one side to the other, through the centre.

Your compass must always be set to half the diameter (radius).

The diameter is indicated on a drawing by the following symbol: **Ø** ie; Ø50

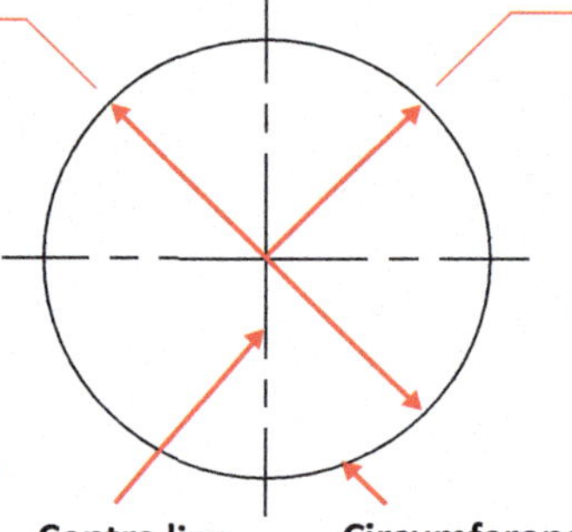

Radius
Is the distance from the centre to circumference.

Your compass must always be set to the radius.

The radius is indicated on a drawing by the following symbol: **R** ie; R25

The Compass

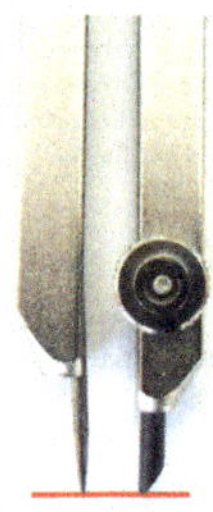

Sharpening
Sharpen the lead on an angle, on the outside edge, on fine sandpaper. *Use an HB lead.*

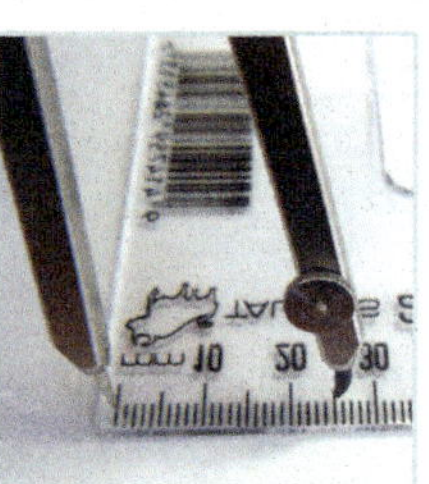

Setting
Place your ruler or set square flat on your desk with the numbered side facing you. You can make a small hole for the compass point to locate into the plastic at the first millimetre mark, then open the leg to the required distance.

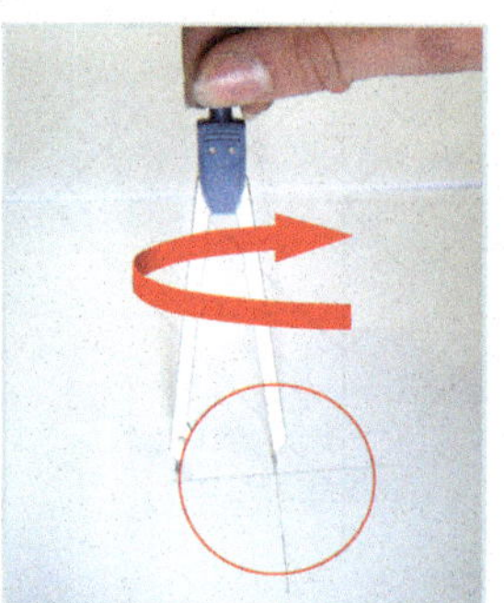

Holding and Using
Draw the centre lines first, as very light construction lines. Where they meet is the place to rest the point of the compass.

Hold the compass between your forefinger and thumb. Lean it on a slight angle away from you and twist it in the direction of the arrow, **drawing the curve only once**. Begin and end the curve at the same place on the centre line. *Practise drawing some circles on a piece of scrap paper.*

ISBN 978-0170185615

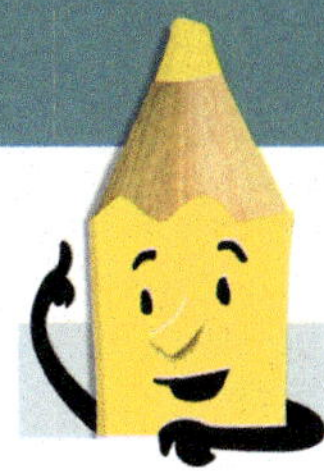

Do the following exercises on **Worksheet 5 Compass Exercises**.

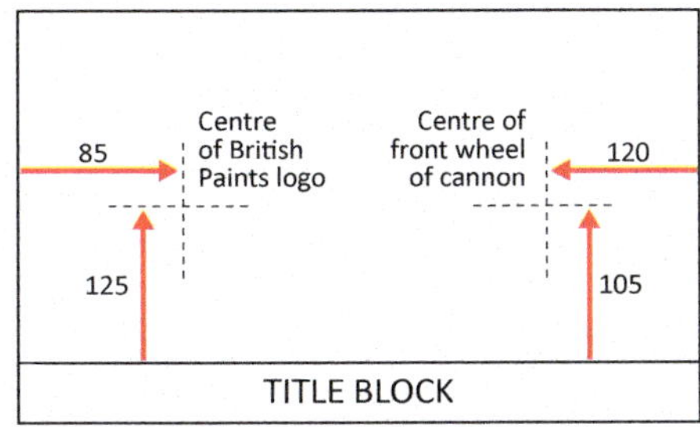

1 Prepare a new title block COMPASS EXERCISES. Use the page layout shown, drawing the centre lines first as construction lines.

2 With a sharp compass, a 2H pencil and your instruments, redraw the British Paints logo and the Toy Cannon.

3 Use colouring pencils and your 4B pencil to render the Toy Cannon.

British Paints Logo

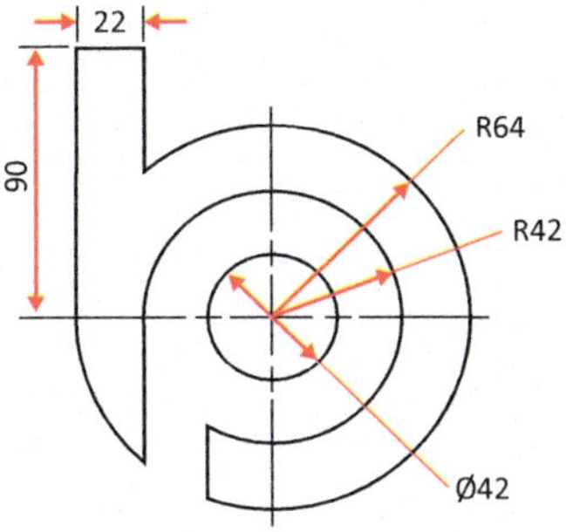

22
90
R64
R42
Ø42

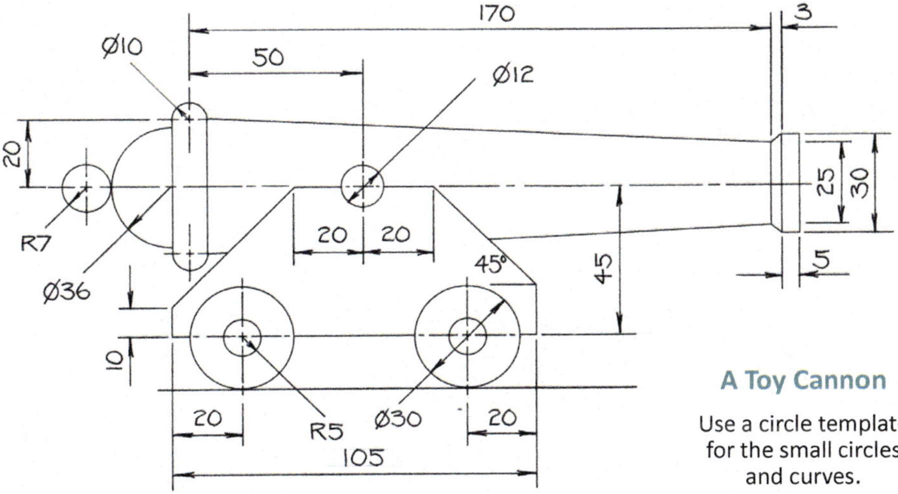

170
3
Ø10
50
Ø12
20
20
20
25
30
R7
Ø36
45°
45
5
10
20
R5
Ø30
20
105

A Toy Cannon

Use a circle template for the small circles and curves.

ISBN 978-0170185615

Toy Cannon Method

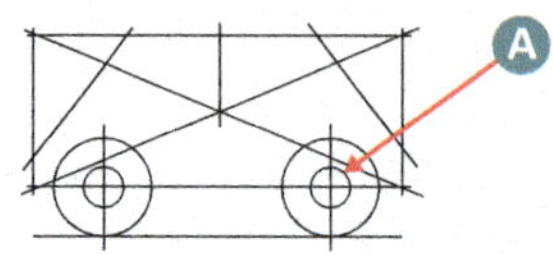

Step 1
Draw the bottom part. Start by locating the centre of, and drawing the wheel at A.

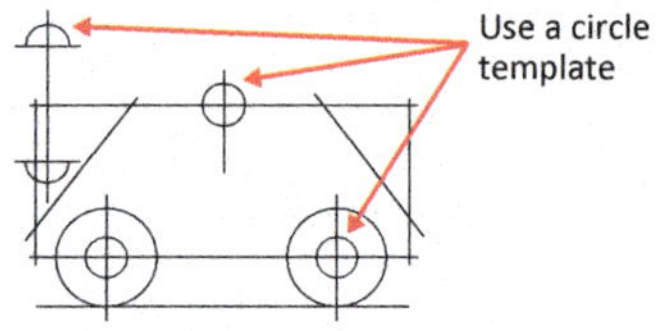

Step 2
Locate and draw the back wheel and small circles and semi-circles.

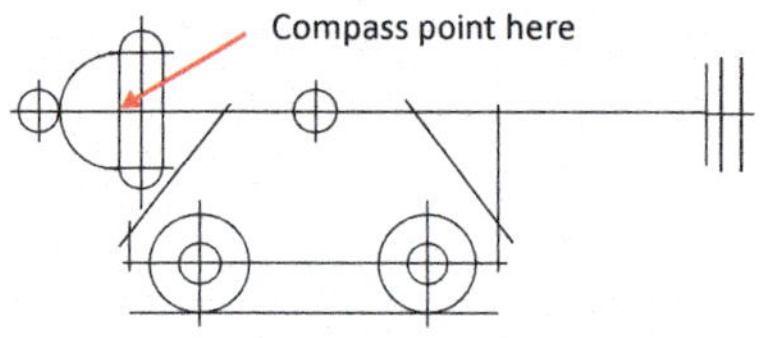

Step 3
Complete the end curves and set out for front of barrel.

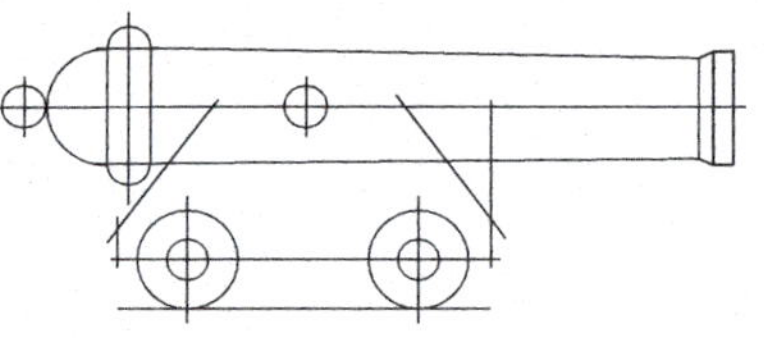

Step 4
Complete the barrel. Check, erase, then outline.

Finishing Your Drawing

Use your colouring pencils and the 'layering' technique *(in this case yellow, brown and orange on top of each other)* to achieve a rustic look to the barrel of the cannon. Keep the colour away from the middle to make it look rounded.

To create the weathering effect on the barrel, use an eraser against the edge of the erasing shield to make light, vertical stripes by removing some of the colour. Be sure to keep all the stripes parallel to each other and vertical.

A 4B pencil smudged with a tissue can be used to create the rounded wheels, leaving them white in the centre.

For wood use brown, yellow and orange on top of each other. Add some curved lines on top with a sharp HB pencil to make the wood grain.

Add the shiny effect on the side with an eraser.

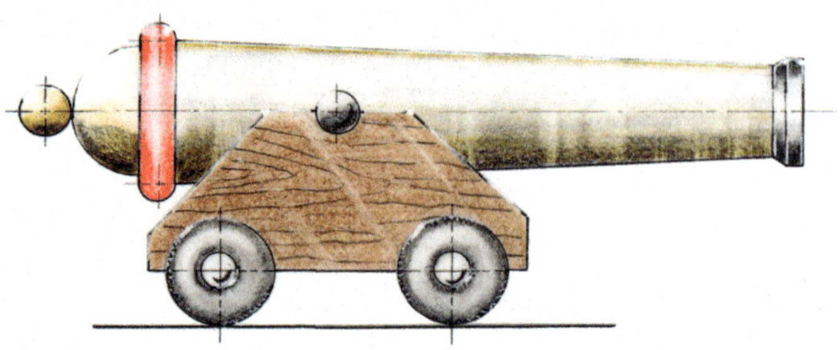

ISBN 978-0170185615

Orthographic Projection

An orthographic projection is a drawing of an object that shows three or more views of the different sides, when looking directly at them, and then drawn in set positions to make one complete drawing. The name comes from the Greek **orthos** (meaning right) and **gonia** (meaning angle). An orthographic projection is sometimes called a *working drawing*. An orthographic projection is a two dimensional drawing (2D).

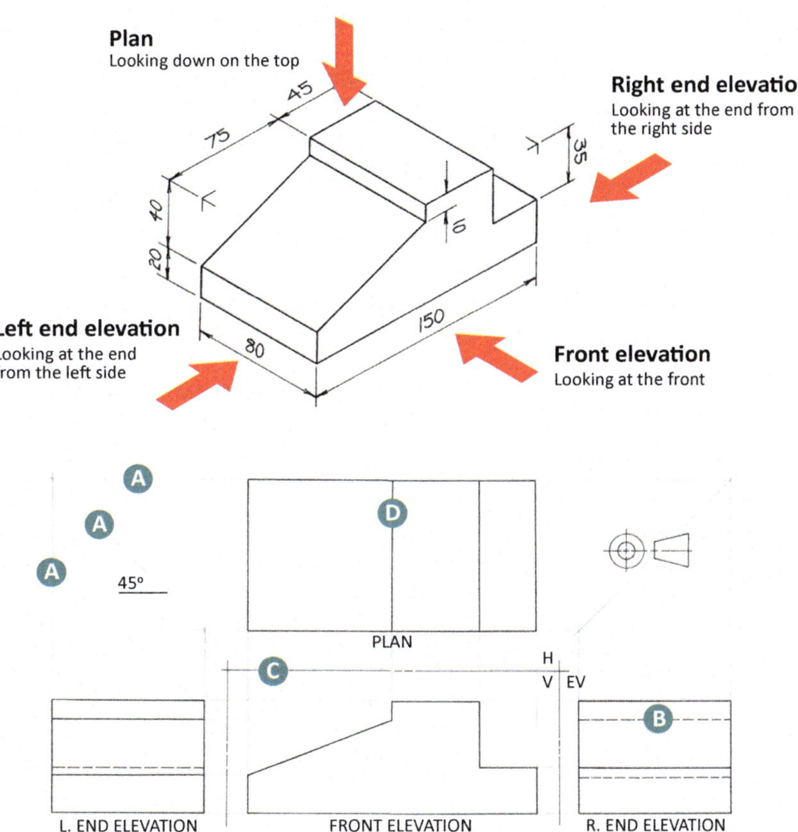

There are three types of lines used on an orthographic projection – light, medium and dark.

- **A** **Construction lines** – very light and thin, 2H pencil.
- **B** **Hidden detail** – slightly darker than construction lines (medium) and thin, 2H pencil.
- **C** **Reference lines** – the same darkness as hidden detail (medium) and thin, 2H pencil.
- **D** **Outlines** – dark, sharp and thin, 2H pencil. Twist the pencil as you draw.

ISBN 978-0170185615

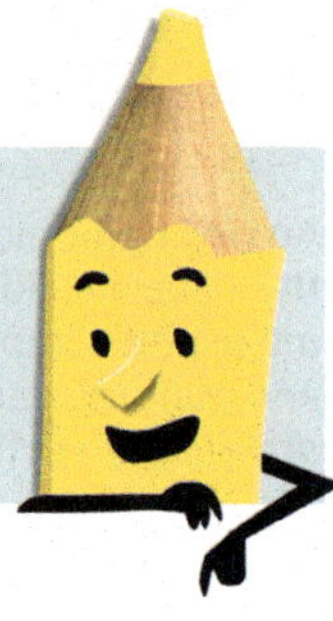

On **Worksheet 6 Orthographic Projection 1**, prepare a new title block ORTHOGRAPHIC PROJECTION, then draw the object shown on page 23. Follow the steps below to set it out.

Remember to make all your lines very light construction to begin with, using a sharp 2H pencil.

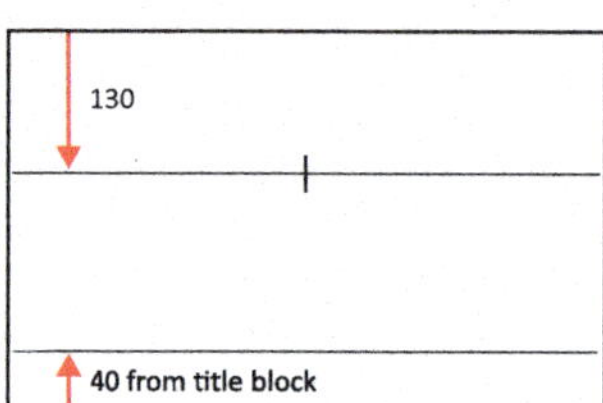

Step 1

1 Set out two construction lines on which the PLAN and ELEVATIONS will rest.

2 Because there will be two end elevations, the plan will be in the centre of the page. Find the CENTRE of the top line. Mark it with a light dash, not a dot.

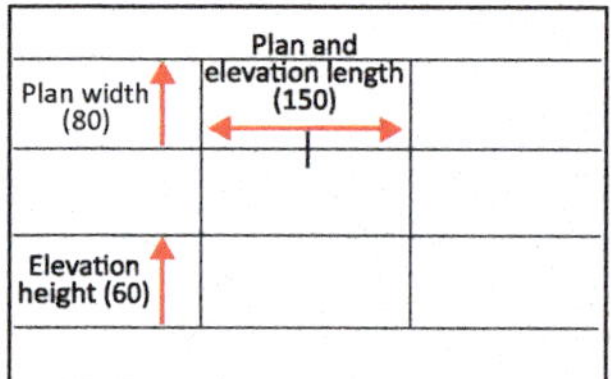

Step 2

1 Draw the width of the PLAN (80 mm) and the height of the FRONT ELEVATION (60 mm) with two horizontal lines.

2 Step out the length of the PLAN and FRONT ELEVATION 150 mm. Measure half this length each side of the centre and draw two vertical lines.

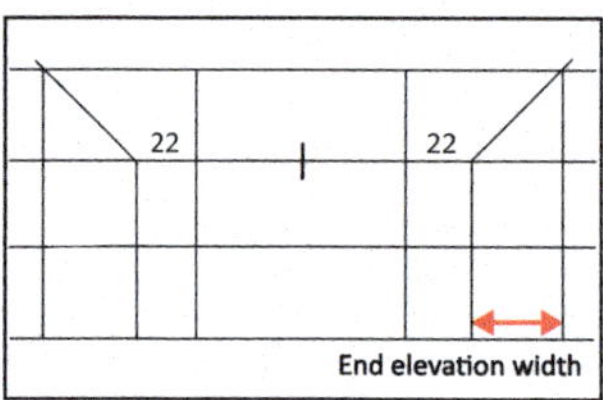

Step 3

1 Measure 22 mm each side of the plan and draw two 45° lines. (This distance will be different on other drawings, depending on the size of the drawing. A good rule is to place the 45° line in the middle of the space between the edge of the plan and the edge of the paper.)

2 Where the 45° lines touch the horizontal lines, project vertical lines down the page for the widths of the end elevations.

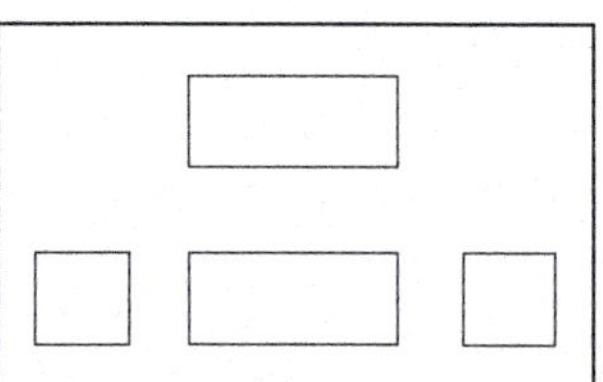

Note that the object shapes are NOT SHOWN HERE. You must get them from the isometric drawing on page 23.

Step 4

1 Draw the shapes of the object inside the four boxes. Begin with the front elevation and project all the other lines from this view through to the other views.

2 Check, then erase unwanted lines, check again, then carefully outline the drawing.

3 Draw the hidden detail and the reference lines, then label the views.

ISBN 978-0170185615

Projection Box

The object to be drawn in orthographic projection is imagined to be placed inside a *projection box*. If the surfaces of the object were projected on to the clear surfaces of the projection box (called planes), which were then opened flat, the arrangement of views would be seen as below.

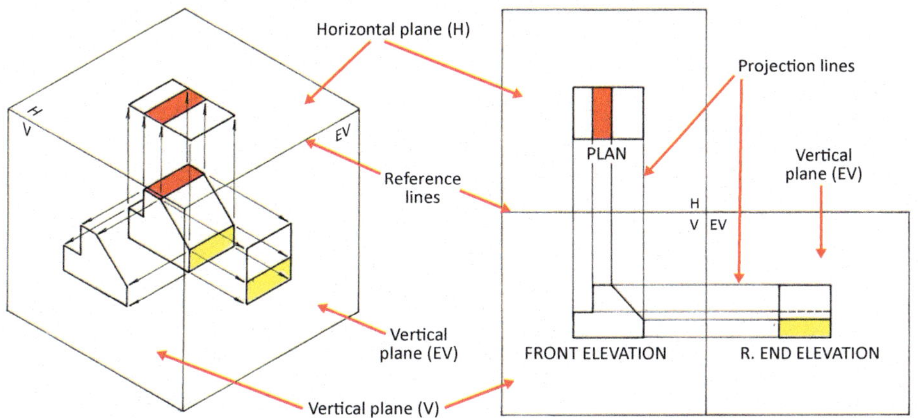

The projection box **The projection box opened flat**

- The plan is directly above and in line with the front elevation.
- The front elevation is directly below and in line with the plan.
- The end elevations are directly in line with the front elevation.
- The views are projected from each other with instruments.

The surfaces that the object is projected onto are called **planes**. There are two planes in a projection box, **horizontal** and **vertical**.

The letters **H** and **V** are used to label the planes in a completed drawing. **EV** is used to label the end elevation planes.

The joins or fold lines between each plane are called the **reference lines**.

Reference lines are a series of long lines broken by two short lines (see page 11).

Reference lines are drawn lighter than outlines with a sharp 2H pencil and should be the same weight and thickness as hidden detail and centre lines (a medium line).

All these specialist lines should be placed on top of the construction lines after the drawing has been outlined.

ISBN 978-0170185615

Projection Symbol

The orthographic drawing you have just drawn is known as 3rd Angle Orthographic Projection. The following symbol should be placed on the drawing to indicate that the drawing is a 3rd angle projection.

The projection symbol is a **truncated cone** lying on its side, viewed from the left side and drawn as a front and end elevation. *Truncated means cut*.

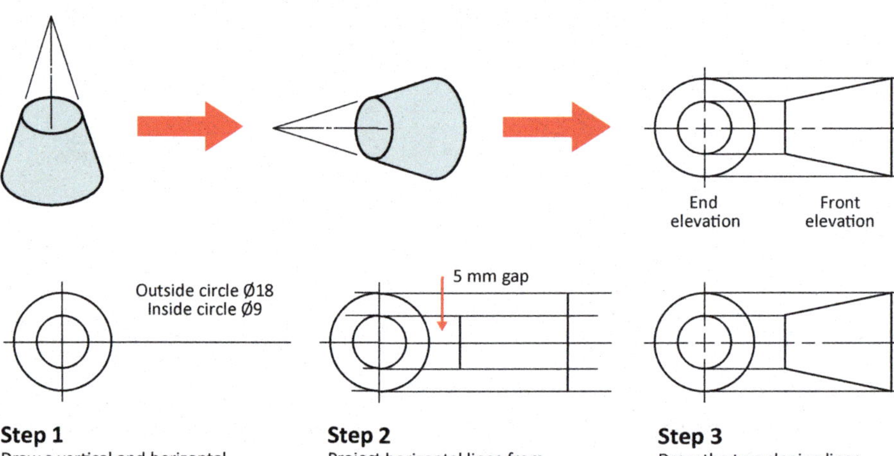

Step 1
Draw a vertical and horizontal construction line. Where they meet draw two circles. Use a circle template.

Step 2
Project horizontal lines from where the circles touch the construction lines. Draw two vertical lines 18 mm apart.

Step 3
Draw the two sloping lines. Erase any lines that overhang and then outline the shape and draw in the centre lines.

The projection symbol may be placed in the title block if there is room, or in a suitable place on the drawing as shown right.

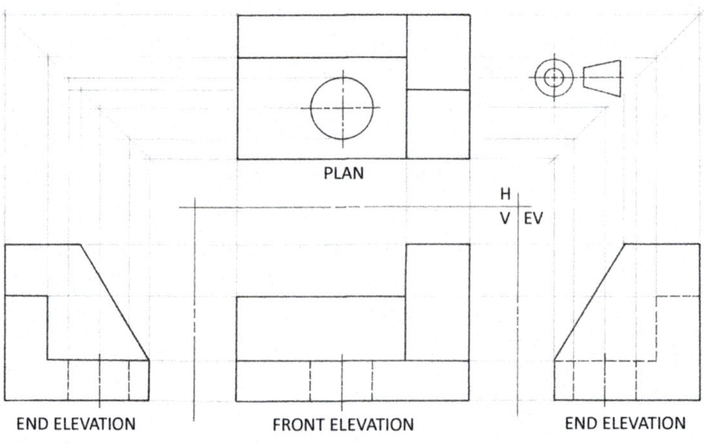

ISBN 978-0170185615

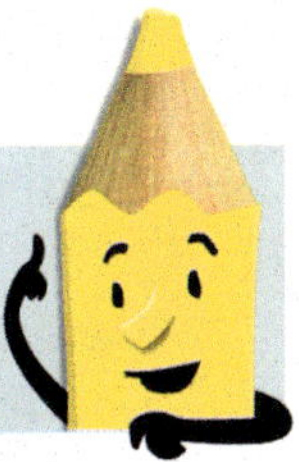

On **Worksheet 7 Orthographic Projection 2**, prepare a new title block SHAPED BLOCK, then draw the object shown below. Follow the same steps you used for the first orthographic projection, but make the first lines **115 mm** from the top of the paper and **35 mm** from the title block.

Remember to make all your lines very light construction to begin with, using a sharp 2H pencil.

Show all the following lines on the drawing: *projection lines, outlines, hidden detail, reference lines, centre lines*. Show the projection symbol and neatly label the views.

When drawing the hole, draw it in the view that shows it as a circle first (the plan) then project the sides of the circle into the other views. They will be straight lines and will show as hidden detail. *(See the previous page. Note centre lines also.)*

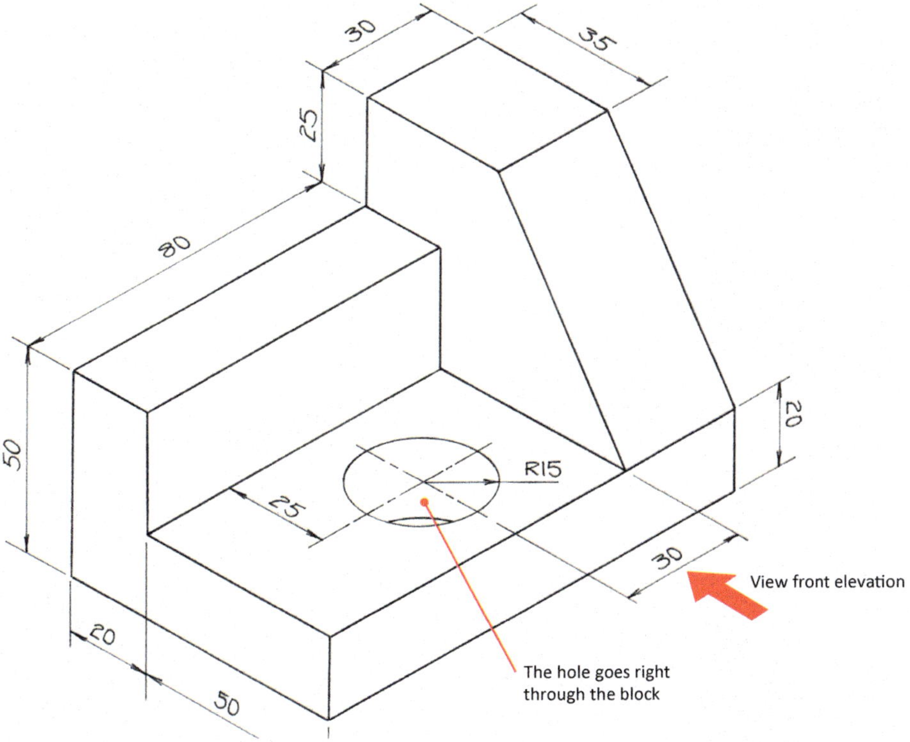

View front elevation

The hole goes right through the block

ISBN 978-0170185615

Tips and Techniques

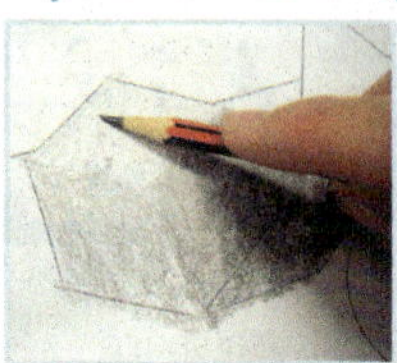

Hold your pencil on a low angle using the side of the lead, not the point. Make your strokes **parallel to the side of the object**.

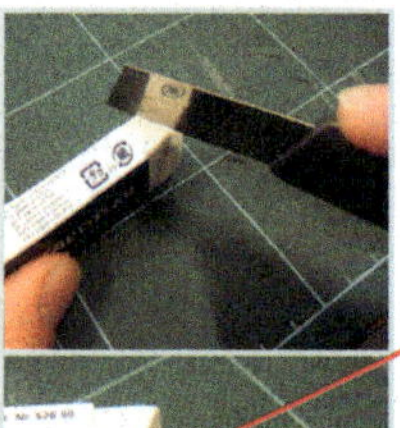

Sharpening your eraser with a craft knife. Note that the eraser is **resting on its side**. Hold it firmly!

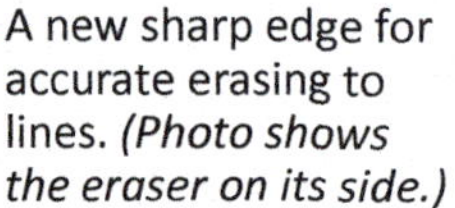

A new sharp edge for accurate erasing to lines. *(Photo shows the eraser on its side.)*

Use the cut off piece for creating highlights on edges and surfaces.

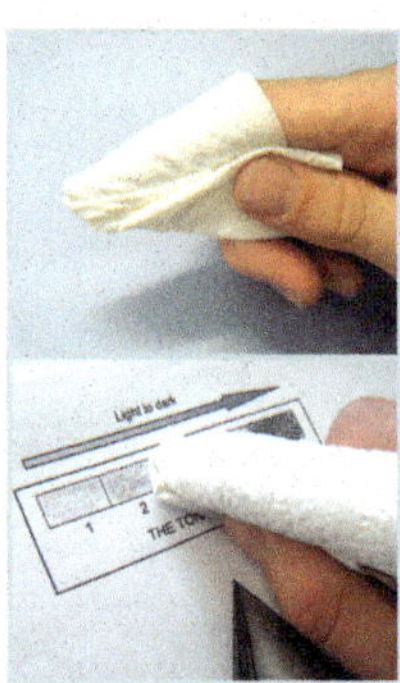

Wrap some tissue around your finger for smudging.

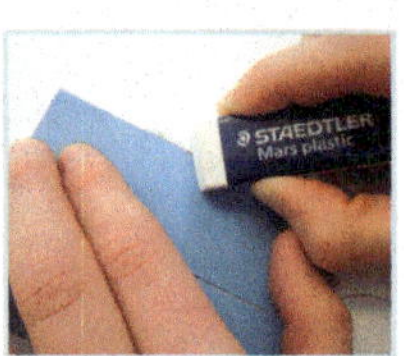

Use a paper erasing shield. Stretch it firmly between you index finger and thumb as you work the eraser against it.

Tone

When light falls on an object, the side facing the light will appear much lighter than the side which is facing away from the light. These lighter and darker versions of the same colour are called **tone**.

Using a soft leaded pencil (4B) is the easiest way to show tone on a drawing. By varying the pressure on the pencil many different tones can be made, from the lightest (almost white) to the darkest (black). Between these will be a range of *mid tones* of different greys.

The tonal scale rectangle on Worksheet 8, for you to complete, is shown below. Use your 4B pencil, a tissue for smudging, an eraser and an erasing shield for sharpening the outside edges. Continue the exercises on page 29 on the same sheet.

Step 1
Render boxes 1, 3 & 5.

Step 2
Render the mid tones 2 & 4.

Step 3
Blend together by smudging with a tissue. Clean up the edges with an erasing shield.

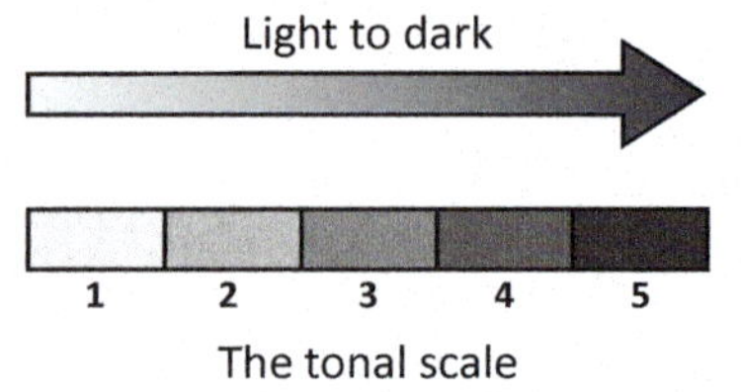

The tonal scale

ISBN 978-0170185615

Before rendering the solids, determine the direction of light ie; from the top left corner.

Divide the solids into imaginary parts as shown in the diagram.

The numbers on each part relate to the tonal scale. This will determine how dark each part will be.

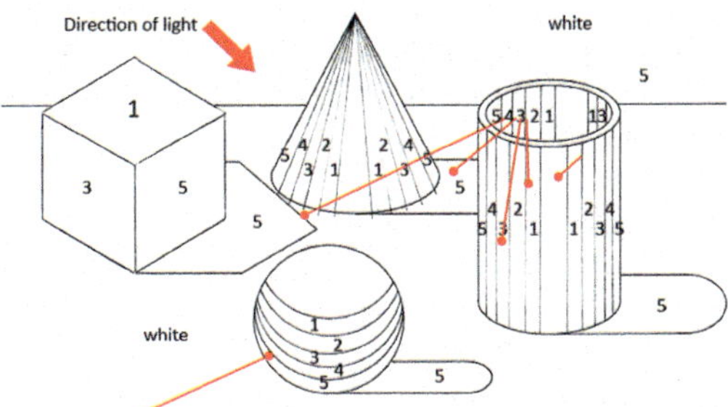

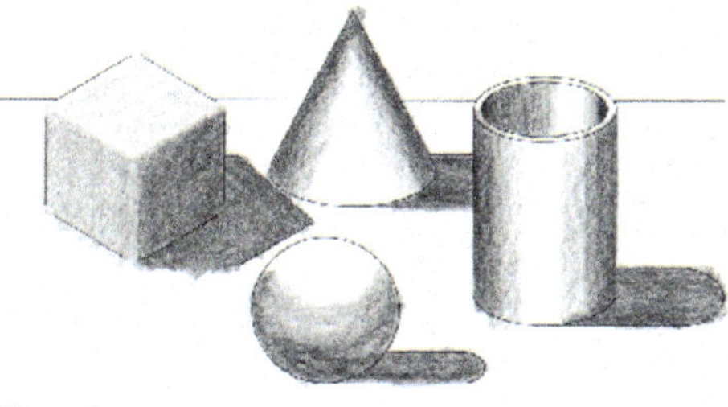

Step 1
Apply 4B pencil to the surfaces, working parallel to the edges and circular on the sphere.

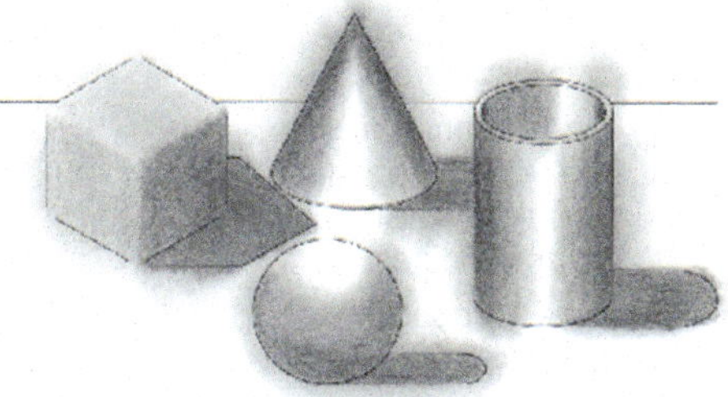

Step 2
Smudge the 4B pencil tones with a tissue, working parallel to the edges and circular on the sphere.

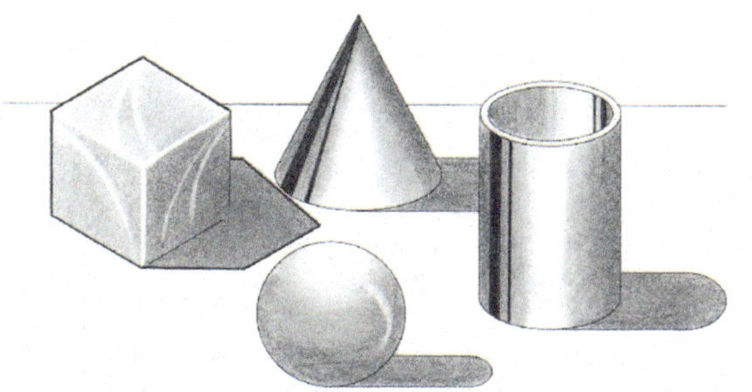

The final rendering shows the drawing cleaned up with an eraser and erasing shield.

Note:

- A thick line around the objects (shown on the cube).
- White highlights applied with an eraser (shown on the surfaces of the cube and sphere).
- Dark stripes on the cone and cylinder to add visual interest (must be parallel to edges).

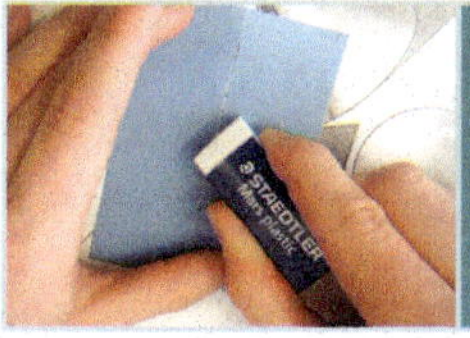

Make an erasing shield with a thin slot to make the sharp, white edges of the cube.

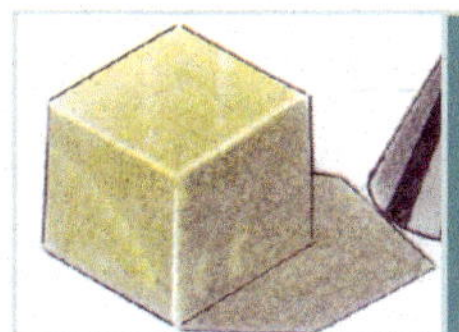

Coloured pencil can be used to apply a colour on the top of the 4B tone.

ISBN 978-0170185615

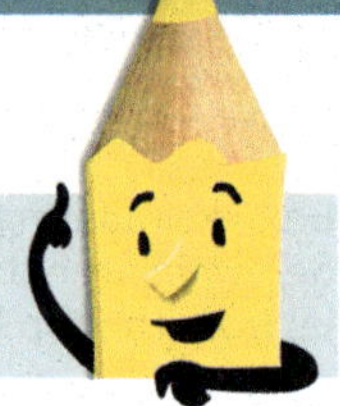

On **Worksheet 10 3D Freehand Sketching**, prepare a new title block FREEHAND SKETCHING, then draw the objects shown on pages 30–32.

These exercises introduce the importance of crates to obtain singular proportion. The crates should be left light but visible about each sketch. Note the following:

- All lines are **freehand**, without the use of your instruments.
- Keep turning the page around so that you are always making horizontal lines.
- Use a 4B pencil.
- Lines should be very light construction to begin with.
- Work slowly and accurately.
- Draw a crate the overall size first.
- Make all lines of the crates parallel to each other.
- Cross the diagonals on the end to locate the centre A.

Leave the crate visible when you have outlined the sketches.

Initial crating

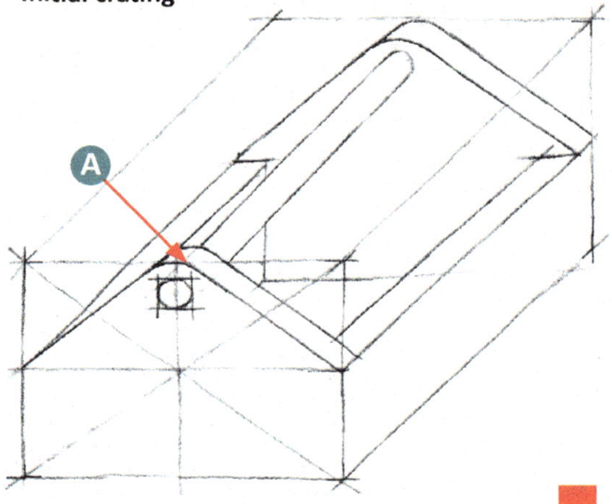

Final rendering

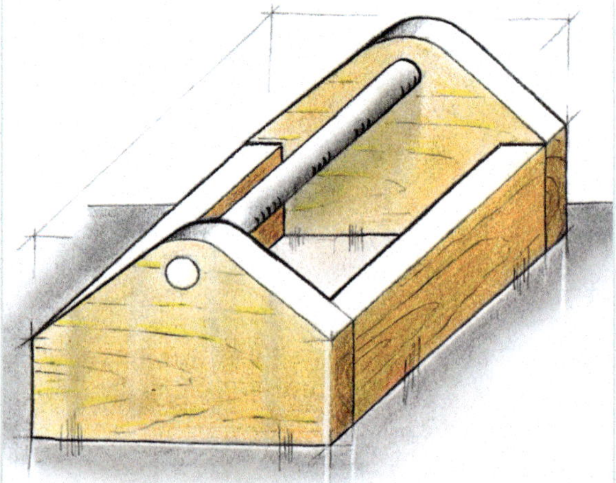

ISBN 978-0170185615

Initial crating

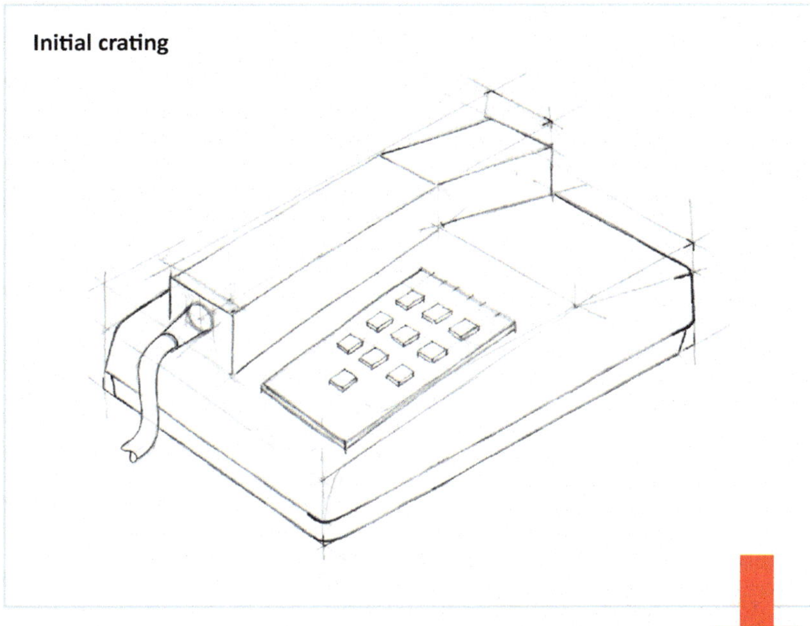

Final rendering

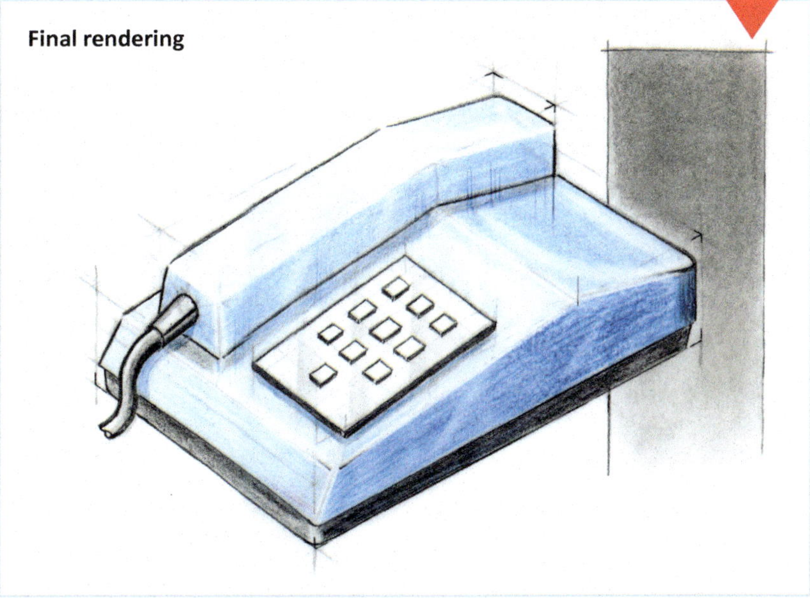

ISBN 978-0170185615

Finishing Your Drawing

Coloured pencil rendering is shown on Matthew's drawing below.

1 A horizon line has been placed behind the tool box to 'anchor' the drawing to the paper.

2 Three different colours on top of each other make the wood of the tool box look real: brown, orange and yellow. *(Use a sharp HB pencil to draw curved lines that represent wood grain.)*

3 Eraser stripes add reflection and visual interest. *(Use an erasing shield to make a sharp edge. The stripes must be vertical on horizontal surfaces.)*

4 Thick lines highlight the outside edges. *(Use a sharp HB pencil.)*

5 Shadows and a background add visual interest. *(Use a 4B pencil smudged with a tissue, edges sharpened with an erasing shield.)*

6 Apply white highlights to edges for added realism. *(Use an eraser and erasing shield as shown on page 29.)*

Take your time to try and make your drawings look as real as possible.

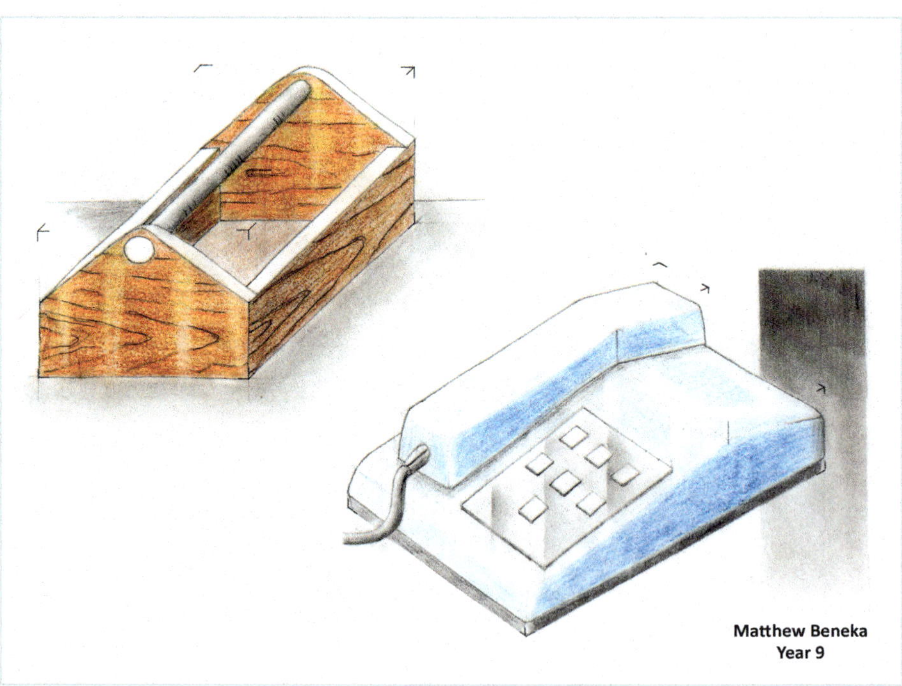

Matthew Beneka
Year 9

ISBN 978-0170185615

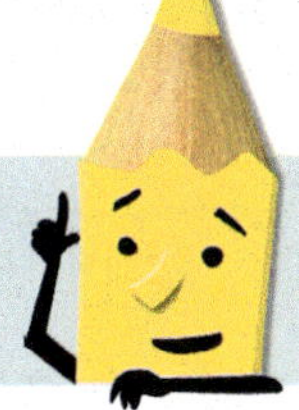

Freehand sketches are drawings that are done without using any instruments. Complete **Worksheet 11 2D & 3D Freehand Sketching** using the guidelines below.

Tips and techniques

- Use a soft pencil (4B) held on a low angle.
- Unclip the paper from your drawing board. Place it on the flat desk top so you can turn it around as you work.
- Use an arm movement, not a wrist movement. *(A wrist movement will give you a curved line instead of straight.)*
- Turn your paper around to draw vertical and angled lines as horizontal lines.
- When sketching 30° and 45° lines, keep the angles low.
- Take your time to sketch each line accurately and **parallel to each other**.
- Put your pencil on the beginning of the line then look ahead to the end of the line as you draw it.
- Make the lines overhang at the corners to give a more 'fluid' look to the sketch.
- Use the same drawing sequence as you would with instruments ie; draw the axes first. Make your sketches larger rather than smaller.

2D Freehand Sketches (Hall Table)

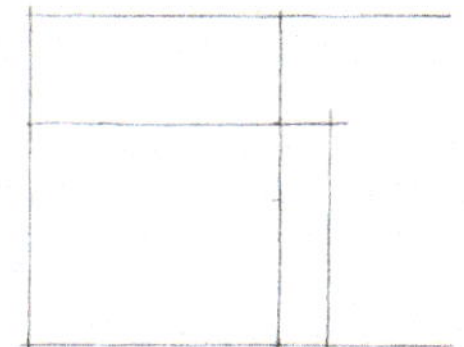

Step 1
Carefully sketch the lines of each crate parallel to each other.

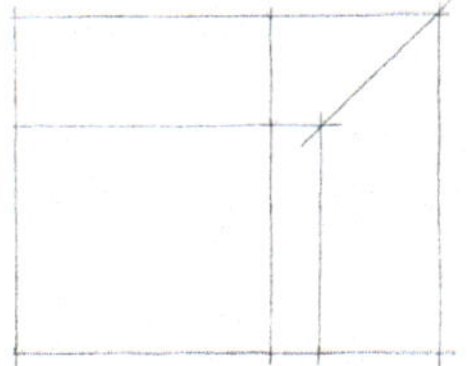

Step 2
Sketch the 45° projection line and outside of the end elevation.

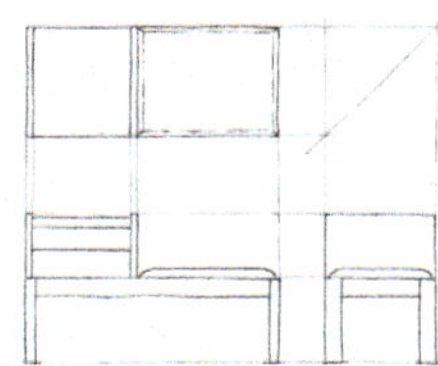

Step 3
Sketch the top of the elevations. Draw the shape inside the crates.

3D Freehand Sketching Guidelines

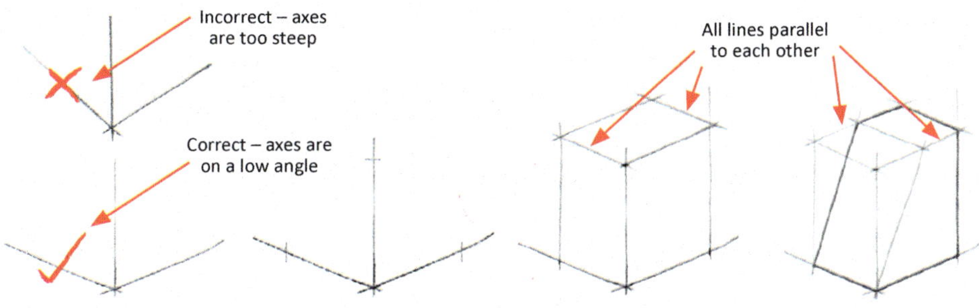

Step 1
Sketch the sloping axes on a low angle using light construction lines.

Step 2
Set out the length of the crate along each axis.

Step 3
Carefully sketch the crate making all the lines parallel to each other.

Step 4
Carefully sketch the object inside the crate. Make the outside lines a thick line.

ISBN 978-0170185615

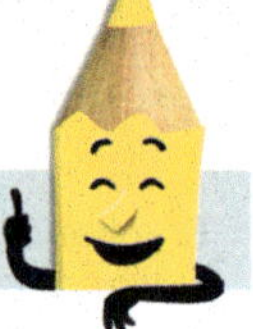

Use the information here to help you complete **Worksheets 13 & 14**.

Detailed sketches show how an object or design will be made or how it will work. These sketches are usually shown on design development pages of a design assignment, to convey the ideas of a designer more clearly. Two types of detailed sketches are *exploded isometric* (3D) and *sectioned* (2D) sketches.

3D Exploded Isometric Sketches

Freehand exploded isometric sketches show the object pulled apart.

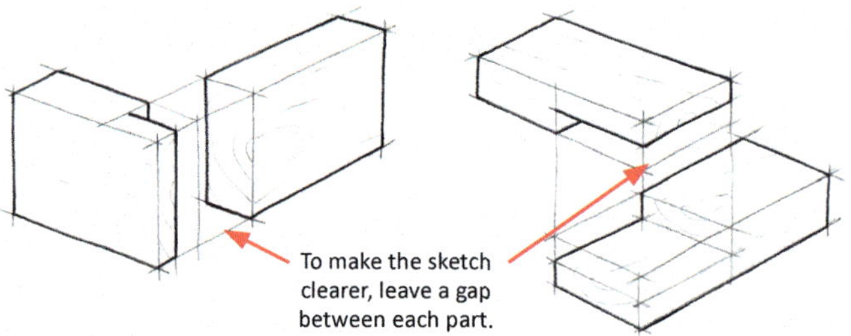

The answers to the wood joints on Worksheet 13 are shown. Begin by drawing the axes first, then the crates, then the shape of the wood joint inside. Tip: Sketch the joint assembled first, then show it pulled apart in the direction it would be assembled. Draw a thick outline around each.

2D Sectioned Sketches

Freehand sectioned sketches show what an object looks like inside. This is done by *sectioning*, which is imagining the object has had a part removed or cut off. The surface that is imagined to be cut is 'hatched' with 45° lines. Different parts of the object are hatched in opposite directions.

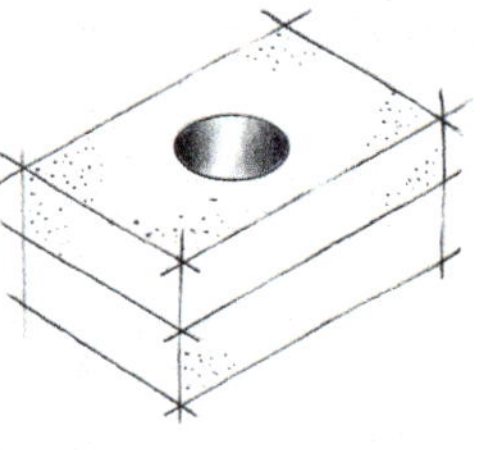

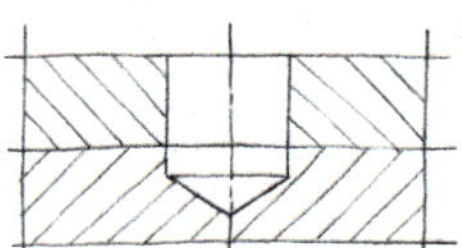

The sectioned sketch above shows that the hole does not go all the way through the object shown at left.

2D sketches can be a complete orthographic projection showing a plan and front and end elevations, or a one view sketch. The sectioned 2D sketch of the torch on **Worksheet 14** is shown below. Although it is not entirely accurate, and the batteries have not been shown, it does give a good indication of the internal detail.

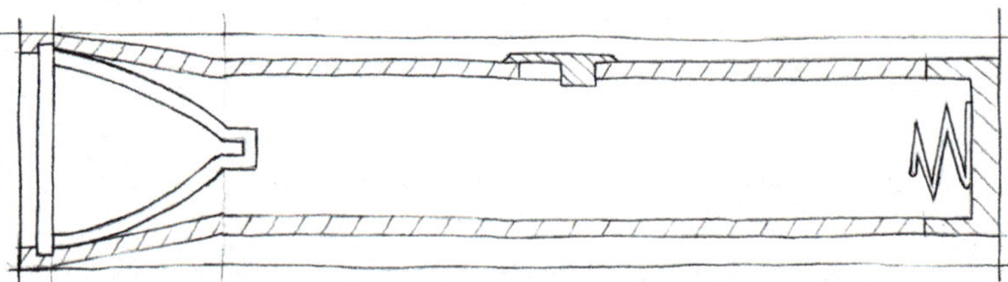

ISBN 978-0170185615

Oblique Drawing

The word oblique means **angle**. An oblique drawing is a way of showing an object pictorially. The entire object is shown in one drawing when looking directly from the front and down onto the top and one side.

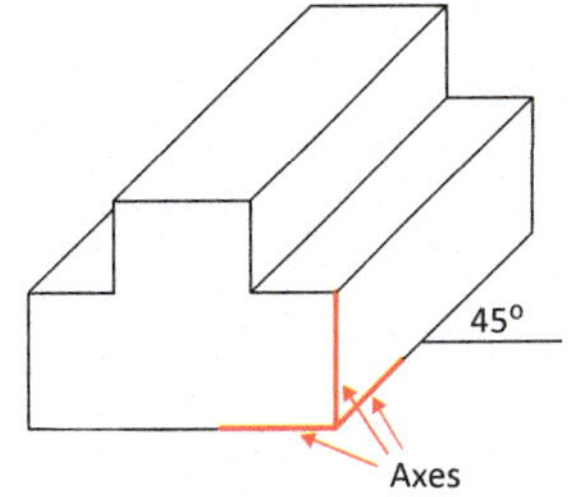

An oblique drawing is a three dimensional drawing (3D).

There are three main lines in an oblique drawing, horizontal, vertical and sloping, called the **axes**. The sloping axes are drawn with your 45° set square.

The axes are always drawn first to make a crate, inside which the shape of the object can be drawn.

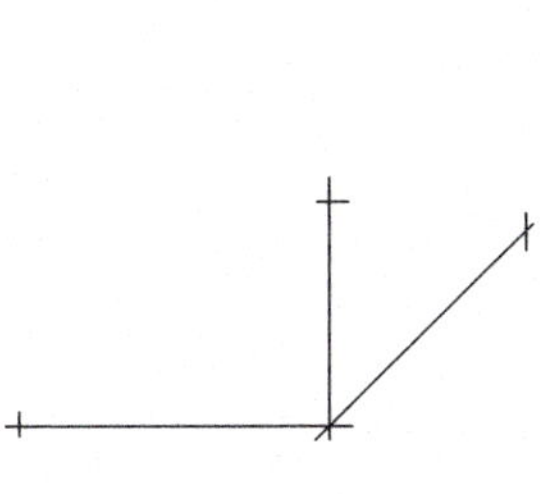

Step 1
Draw the axes in light construction. Measure the overall sizes of the object along the axes.

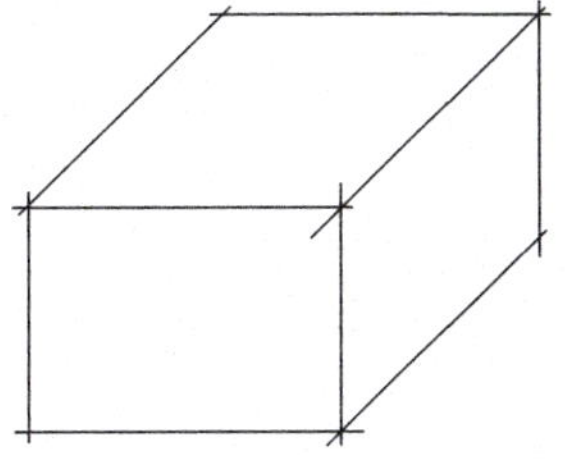

Step 2
Draw the crate that will contain the shape of the object.

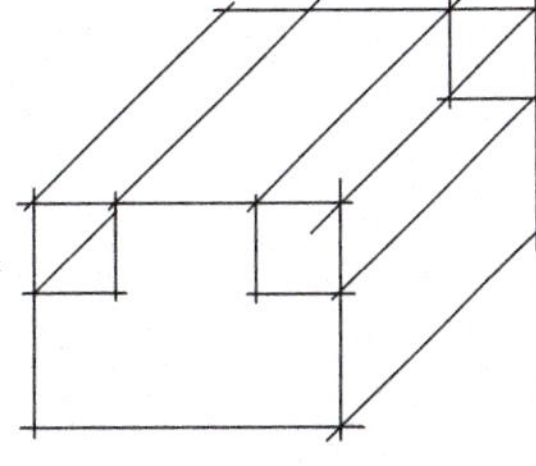

Step 3
Draw the shape of the object inside the crate. Check, erase unwanted lines and outline the drawing.

Draw the Shaped Block and Camera (shown on the next page) on **Worksheet 15 Oblique Drawing.** Prepare a title block OBLIQUE DRAWING and use the page layout shown. Print the names of each object at the top of the page between 4 mm guide lines.

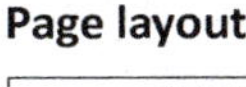

Page layout

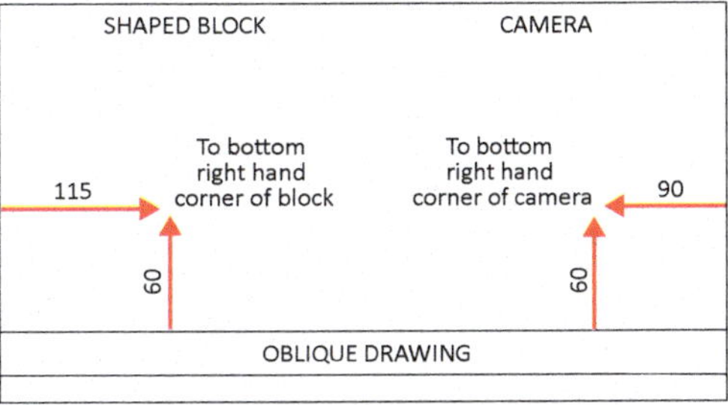

ISBN 978-0170185615

Shaped Block

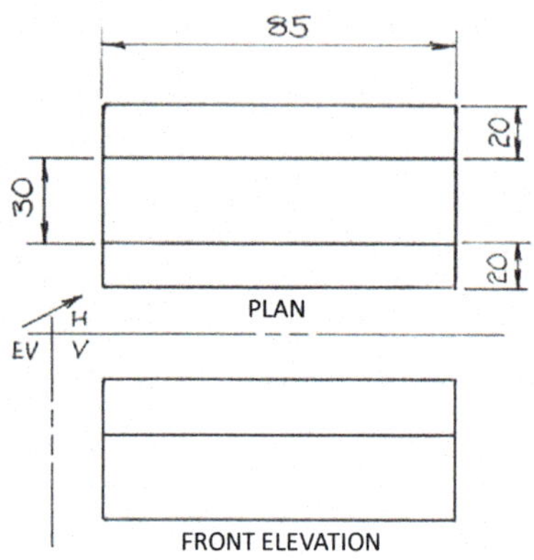

The orthographic projections of the Shaped Block and Camera are given.

View in the direction of the arrow, making the surfaces marked **X** face towards you. (Because you are looking directly at these surfaces they are called the object's TRUE SHAPE.)

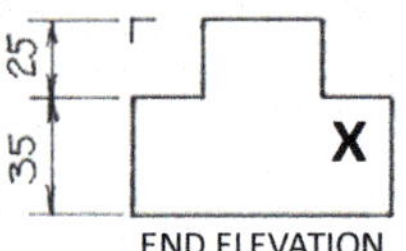

Camera

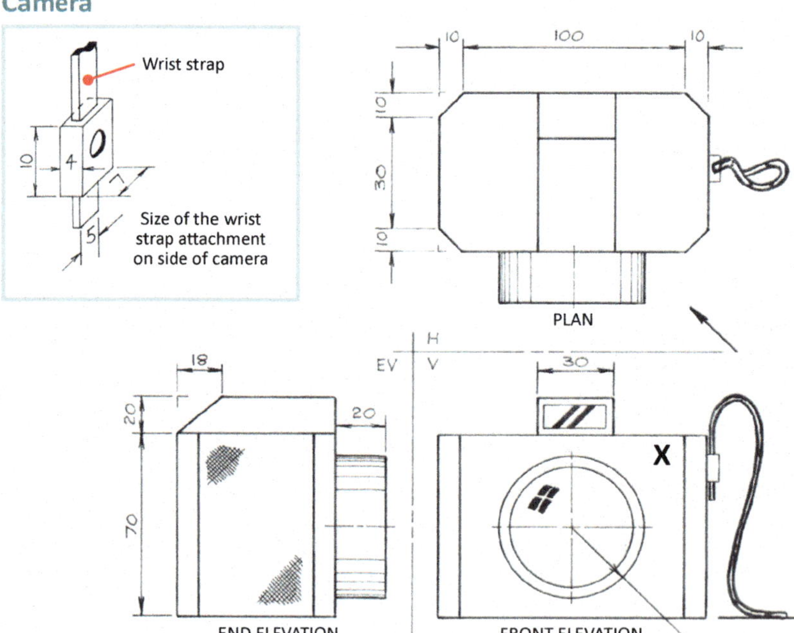

ISBN 978-0170185615

Oblique Camera Method

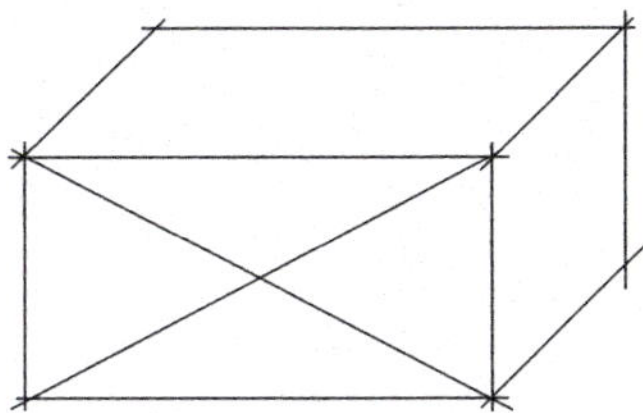

Step 1
Draw the axes and then a crate. Cross the diagonals of the front to find the centre for the lens.

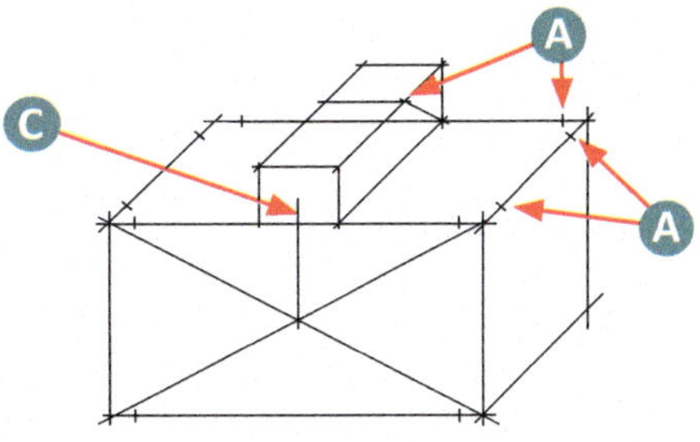

Step 2
Draw the view finder in the middle of the top. Set it out equal either side of the centre at C. Measure along the top axes for the angles at A.

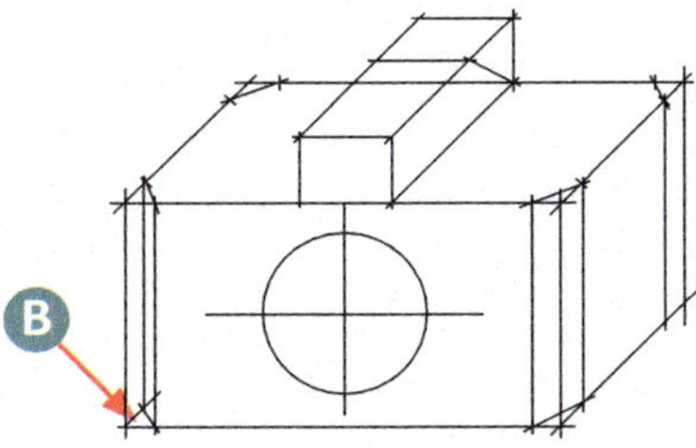

Step 3
Draw the back of the lens as a circle and draw the front corners on an angle. Erase the diagonals. Note line B which is needed to find the bottom of the vertical edge.

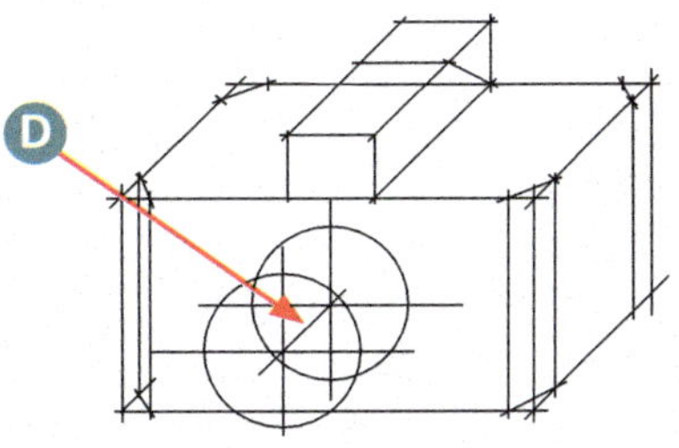

Step 4
Draw a 45° line from the centre of the back circle D and measure along it the length of the lens. Draw another circle the same size.

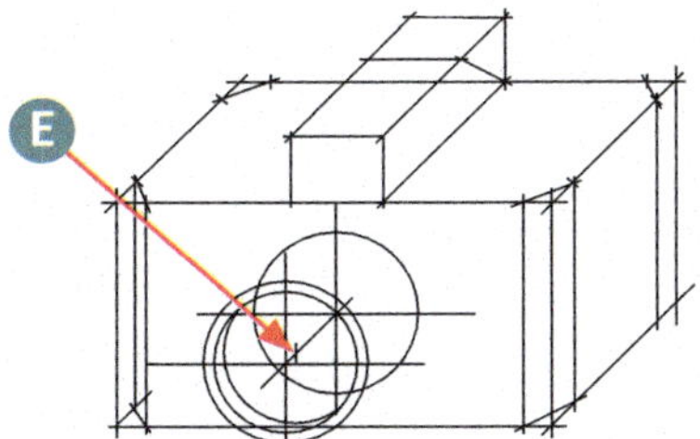

Step 5
Draw another smaller circle inside the front one. Using the same radius, move your compass back along the 45° line a short distance E and draw a part circle for the camera lens.

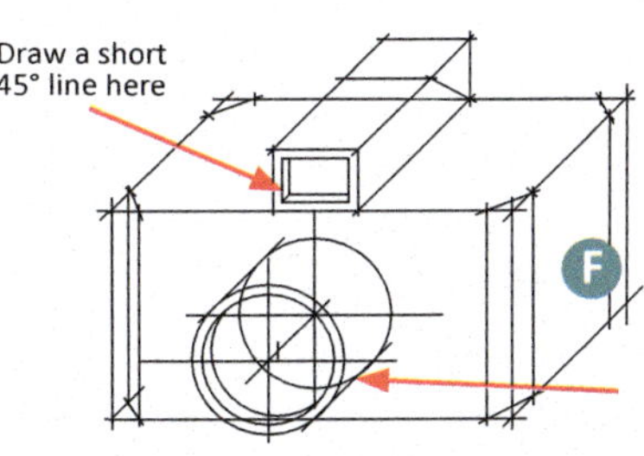

Step 6
Join the circles to make the sides of the lens with two 45° lines F. Complete the front of the viewfinder.

ISBN 978-0170185615

Step 7

To complete the drawing, the strap has been added and the drawing rendered.

- Begin by drawing the box that holds the strap to the camera side A. The sizes are on page 36.
- Sketch the front edge of the curved strap B very lightly freehand until you are happy with the shape. Look closely at the drawing. Then make the other lines parallel to the edge you have just drawn.
- Take care with the curved top, it should be quite narrow.
- Where the strap rests on the surface, and at the top, the lines should be horizontal C.
- The sleeve D is a cylinder.
- Render the strap with a 4B pencil, smudged with a tissue, making it darker where it curves.
- Add a horizon line to anchor the drawing to the page E.

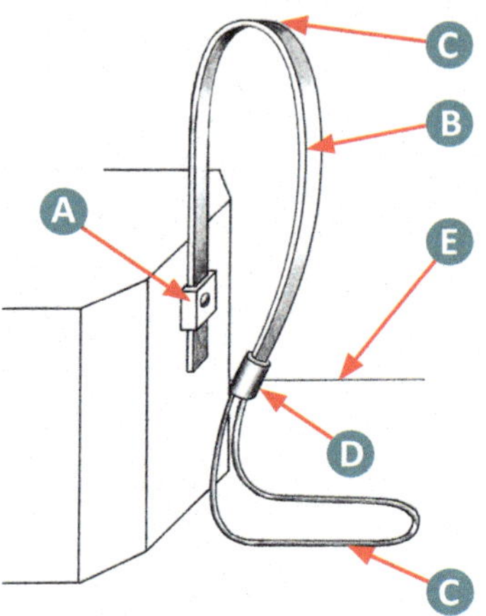

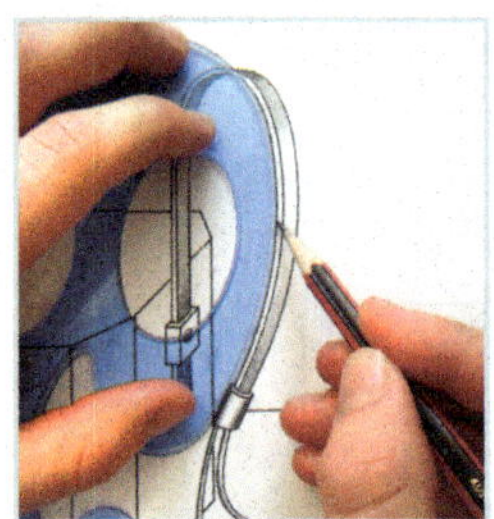

Using a French Curve Template

The photograph left shows a **French Curve** being used to make the curves of the strap accurate. A French Curve is a thin plastic template that has shapes and holes in it that can be drawn around as shown in the photo. If you have access to one it is recommended that you use it. French curves are available from graphic supply outlets.

Here is a view of the lens and Matthew's final drawing showing different rendering techniques that can be applied. Note the centre line (should be lighter than the outlines).

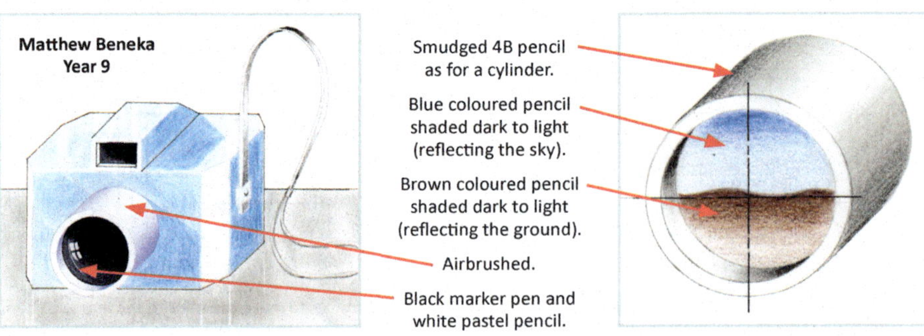

ISBN 978-0170185615

Isometric Drawing

The word isometric means **equal angles**. An isometric drawing is a way of showing an object pictorially. The entire object is shown in one drawing when looking on an angle at the front corner and two sides, and down onto the top. An isometric drawing is a three dimensional drawing (3D).

There are three main lines in an isometric drawing, a vertical and two sloping, called the **axes**. The sloping axes are drawn with your 30° set square.

The axes are always drawn first to make a crate, inside which the shape of the object can be drawn.

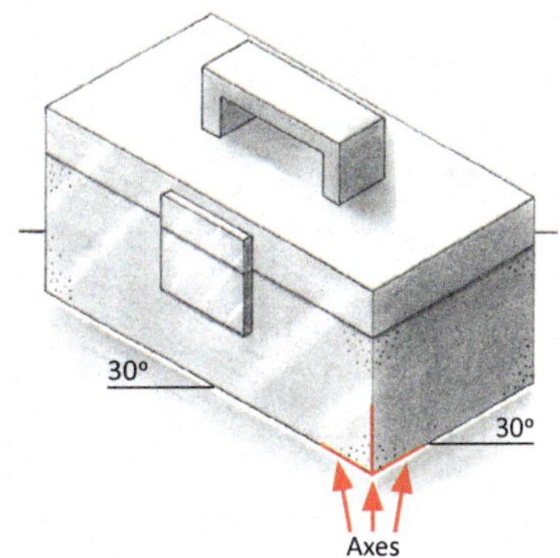

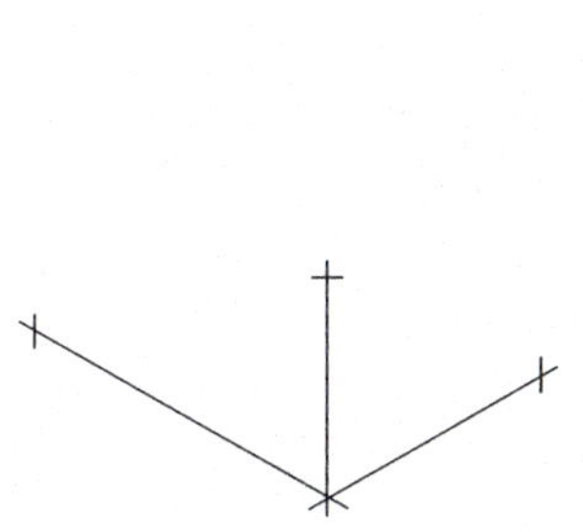

Step 1
Draw the axes in light construction. Measure the overall size of the object along the axes.

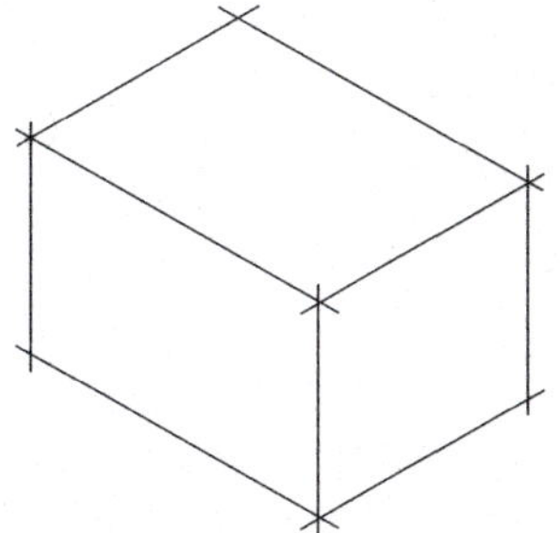

Step 2
Draw the crate that will contain the shape of the object.

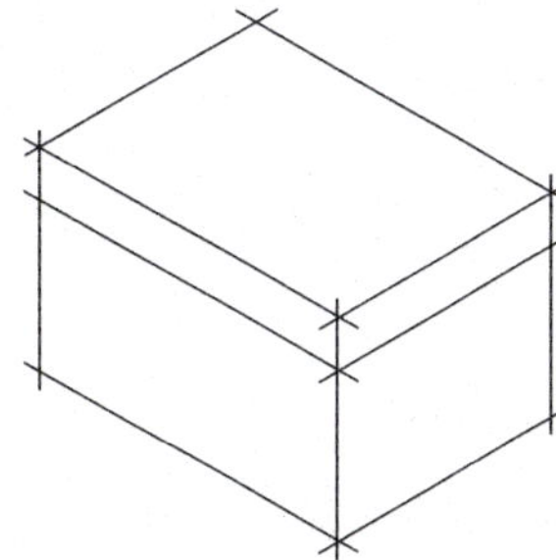

Step 3
Draw the shape of the object inside the crate. Check, erase unwanted lines and outline the drawing.

Draw the Lunch Box and Shaped Block shown on the next page on **Worksheet 16 Isometric Drawing.** Prepare a title block ISOMETRIC DRAWING and use the page layout shown. Print the names of each object at the top of the page between 4 mm guide lines.

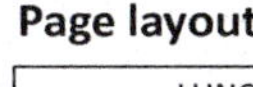

Page layout

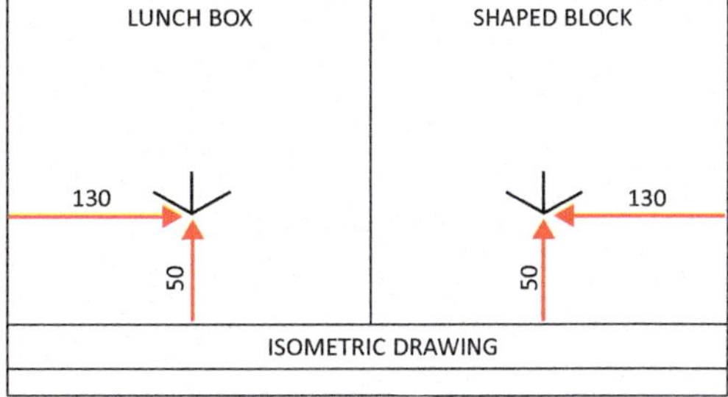

ISBN 978-0170185615

Lunch Box

The orthographic projection of a Lunch Box is shown below. Redraw in isometric when looking in the direction of the arrows. *Judge sizes not given*.

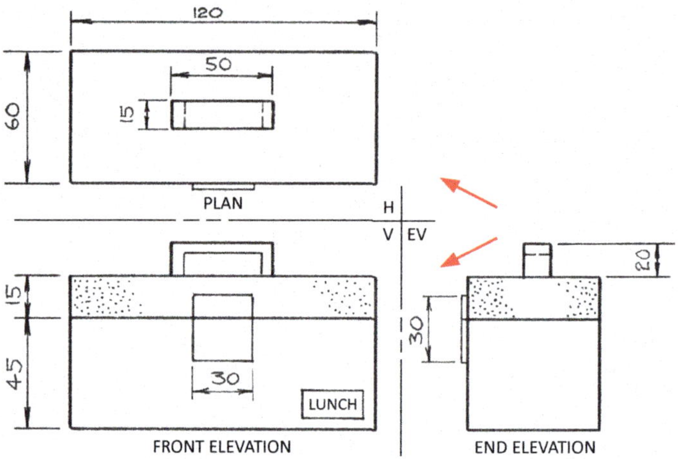

Method

The steps for drawing the handle and catch on the lunch box are shown. Follow them carefully making all lines very light construction to begin with.

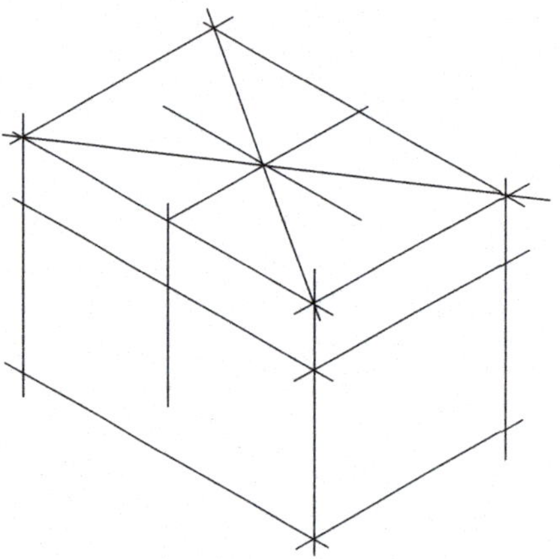

Step 1
Cross the diagonals to find the centre at the top.
Draw the middle lines at the handle and catch.

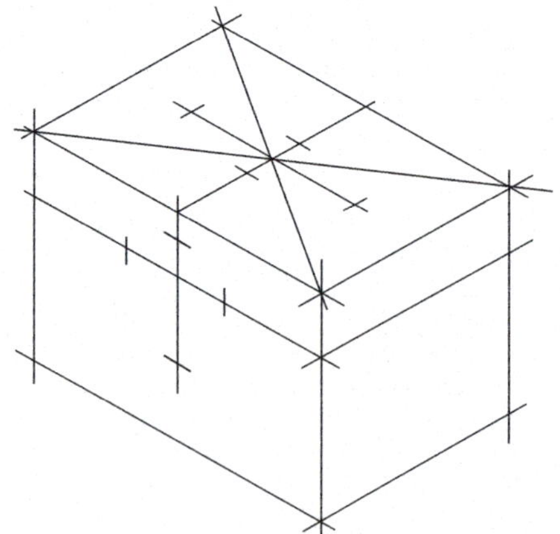

Step 2
Set out half the lengths and widths of the handle and catch, each side of the middle lines.

ISBN 978-0170185615

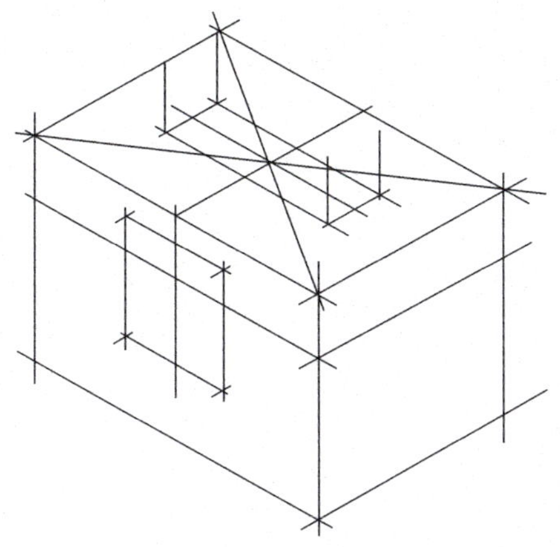

Step 3
Draw the shape of the catch and handle.
Draw the sides of the handle.

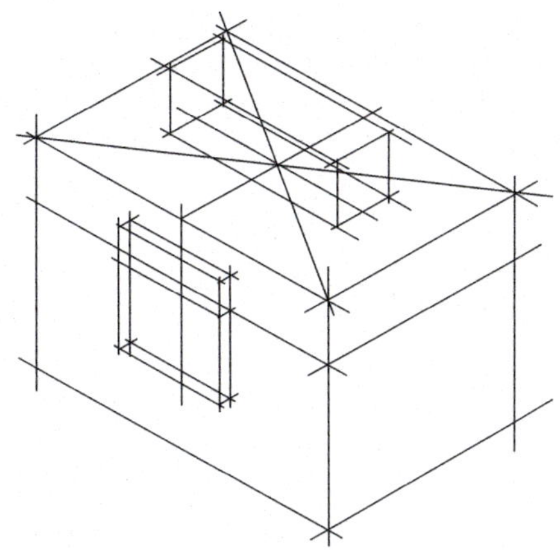

Step 4
Draw the thickness of the catch and the height of the handle. Show a hand grip on the handle as seen on the rendered answer.

Finishing Your Drawing

Suggested coloured pencil rendering of the lunch box is shown at right. Note the white highlights on the front edges and top made with an eraser against an erasing shield.

Practise printing the word LUNCH on an angle as shown below. Then put a box around it to turn it into a badge for the front.

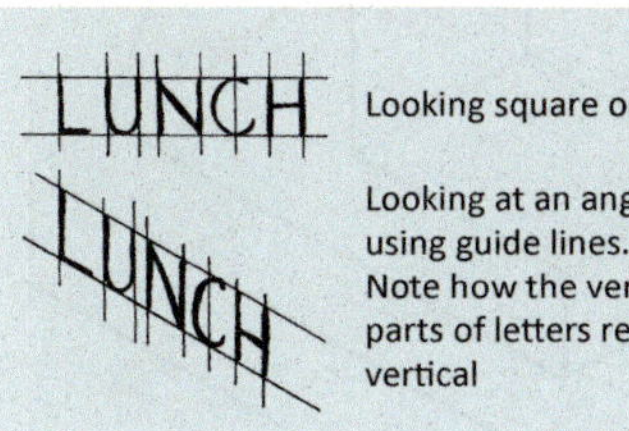

Looking square on

Looking at an angle using guide lines. Note how the vertical parts of letters remain vertical

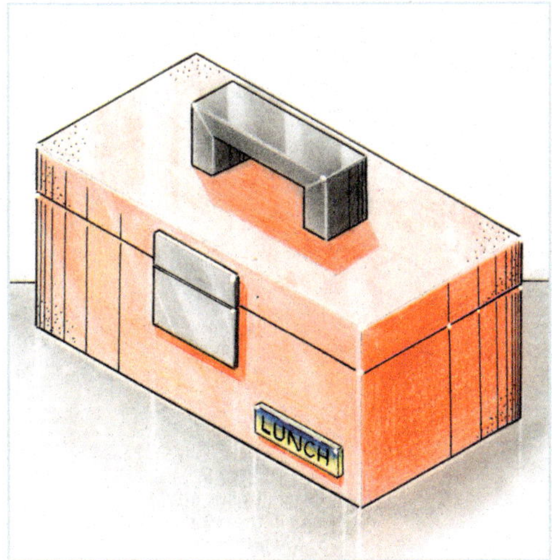

ISBN 978-0170185615

Shaped Block (SCALE 1:4)

The orthographic projection of a Shaped Block is shown below. Redraw in isometric when looking in the direction of the arrows. Note that the block is drawn to a scale of 1:4 (divide all the sides by four). *Judge sizes not given.*

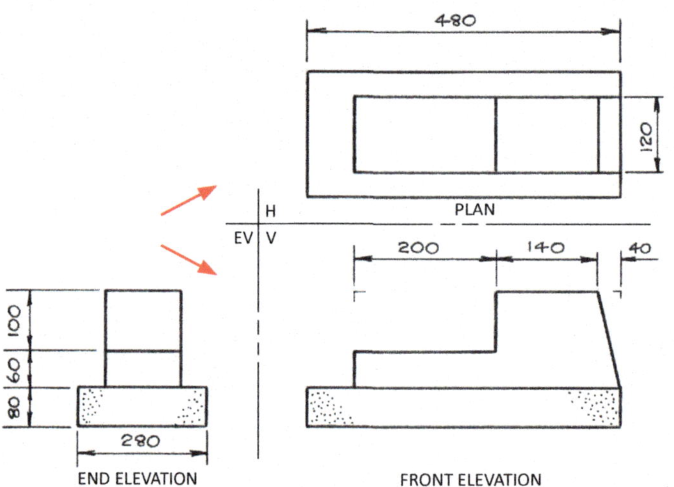

Method

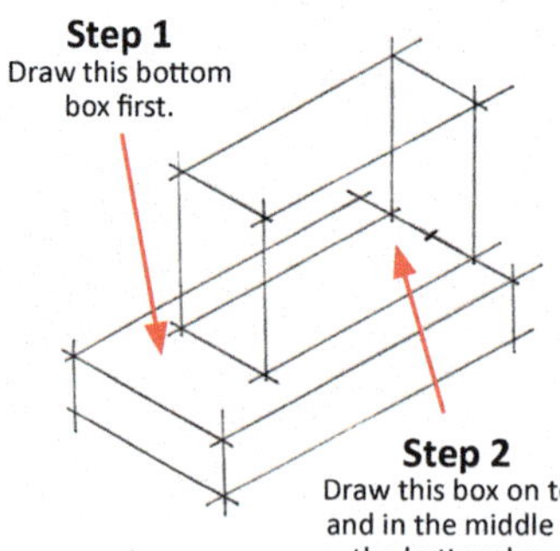

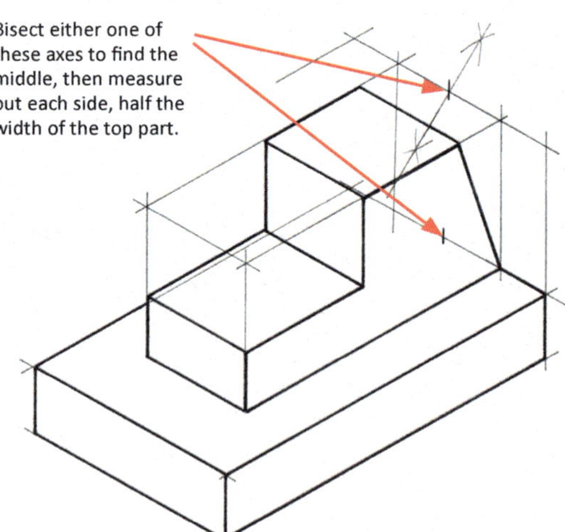

ISBN 978-0170185615

Isometric Circles – The Compass Method

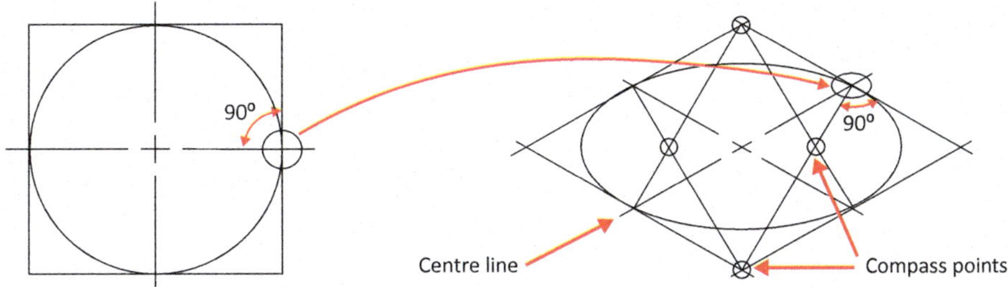

A circle drawn on an angle will no longer be a circle but an oval shape known as an **ellipse**. A circle fits exactly inside a square (above). The compass point for drawing the circle inside the square is found where the centre lines meet. The centre lines are at 90° to the square at the point where they touch the square.

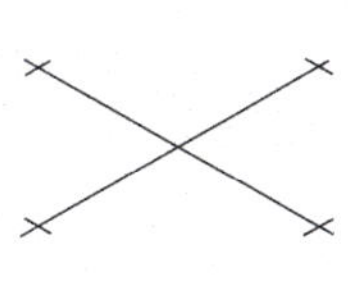

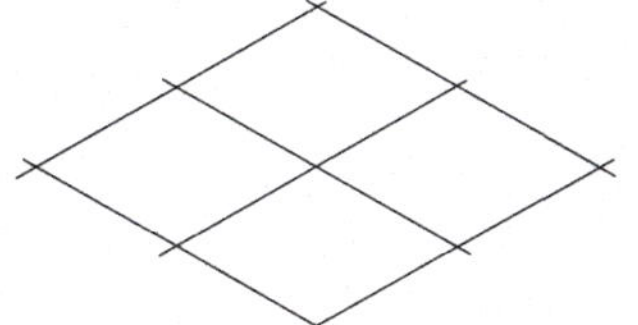

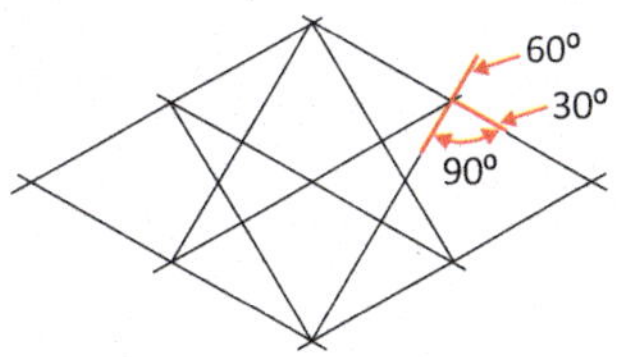

Step 1
Draw the 30° centre lines as construction lines. Set your compass to the radius of the circle and step this distance from the middle along each line.

Step 2
Draw 30° lines parallel to the centre lines through the radius points of each line. This will make the box inside which the circle will be drawn.

Step 3
At each point where the centre lines touch the sides of the box, draw lines at 90° to the sides of the box. Because the box sides are 30°, the lines will be 60° (60° + 30° = 90°).

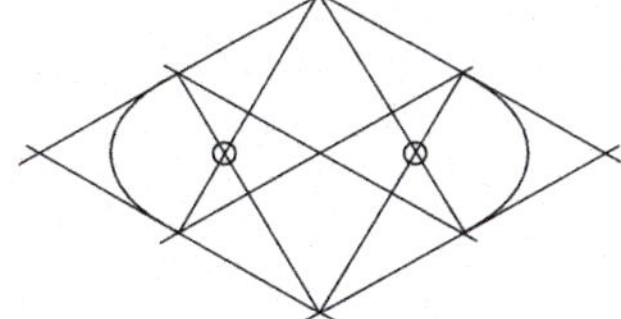

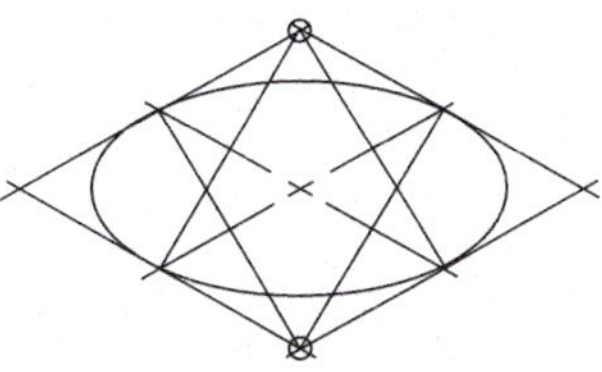

Step 4
Where the 60° lines meet is the compass point (O). Put your compass on each, open it to the length of the line until it touches the side of the box, and draw the two curves that will form the ends of the ellipse.

Step 5
Where the 60° lines meet at the corners of the box (O) are the compass points for the remaining two sides of the ellipse. Put your compass on each, open it to the length of the line until it touches the side of the box, and draw the two curves that will form the rest of the ellipse.

Leave all construction lines very light, outline the circle and place a centre line through it.

ISBN 978-0170185615

Isometric Circles and Curves 17

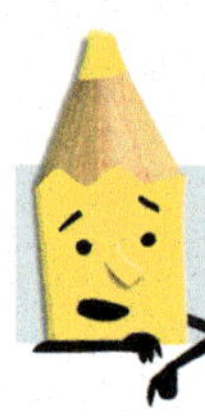

Use the information here to help you complete **Worksheet 17 Isometric Circles and Curves.**

Isometric Cylinder

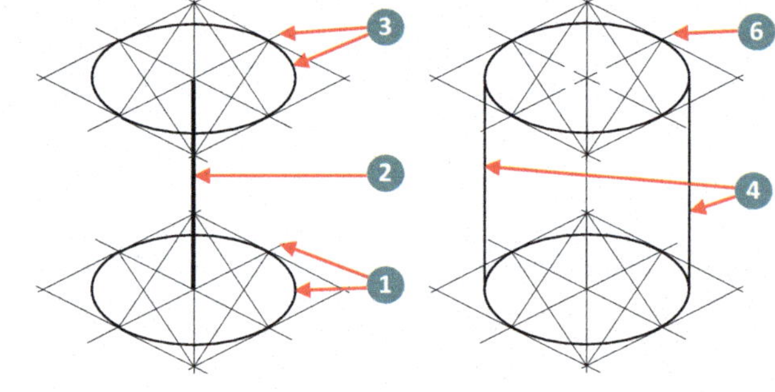

Step 1
Draw the bottom circle as on the previous page.

Step 2
Draw the vertical axis and measure along it the height of the cylinder.

Step 3
Draw the top circle the same as the bottom one.

Step 4
Draw the two vertical sides of the cylinder. The vertical lines will touch the sides of the circles.

Step 5
Check the drawing and outline the cylinder. Leave all the constructions light but clearly visible.

Step 6
Place a centre line through the top circle.

Suitcases Methods

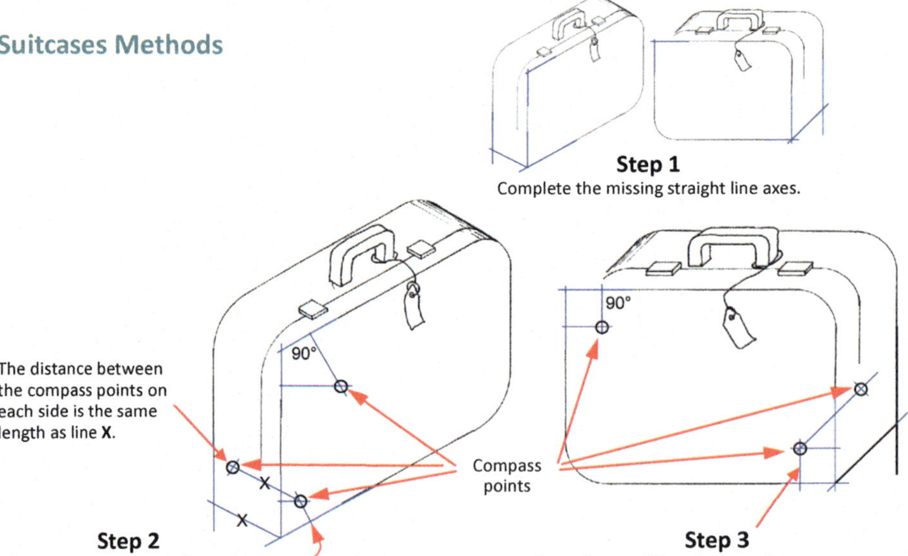

Step 1
Complete the missing straight line axes.

Step 2
Use a compass to step the radius along the axes from the corner.

Step 3
Draw lines at 90° to the axes. Set your compass to the length of these lines and draw the curve.

ISBN 978-0170185615

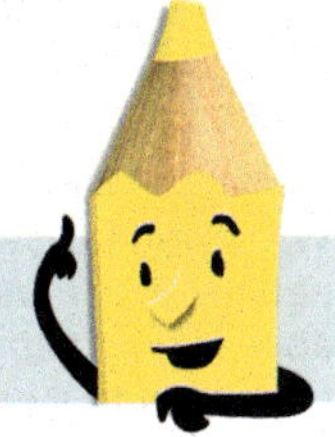

Toy Truck Answer

Use the following guidelines to help you complete **Worksheet 18 Isometric Circles – Toy Truck.**

Put a light construction crate around the front elevation. Then draw the same size crate in isometric.

Use a sharp compass to transfer all sizes from the orthographic projection to the isometric drawing.

Put your compass on point A and open it to the required distances.

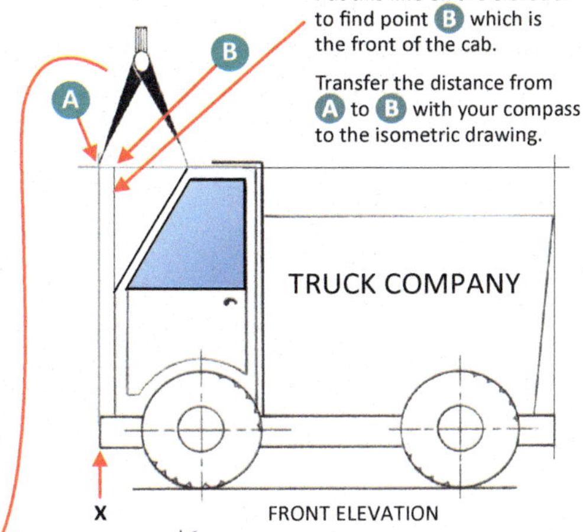

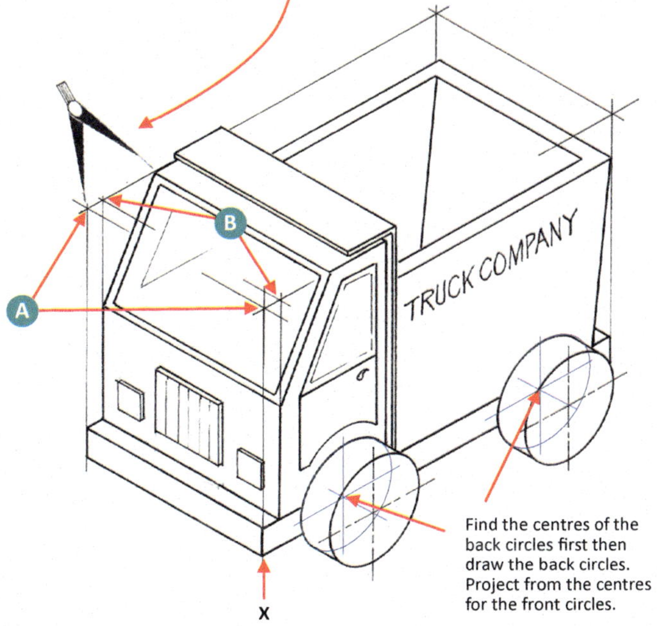

Put this line on the elevation to find point B which is the front of the cab.

Transfer the distance from A to B with your compass to the isometric drawing.

Find the centres of the back circles first then draw the back circles. Project from the centres for the front circles.

ISBN 978-0170185615

Perspective Drawing

When you take a photograph of an object, the resulting image is said to be in perspective. Perspective drawings look realistic, as in a photograph, because objects appear to get smaller the further away they are. The lines of the object also appear to narrow to a point in the distance called the **vanishing point** (VP).

The vanishing point is on the **horizon**, also called the **eye level** line. Lines that travel to the vanishing point are called **visual rays**.

There are two types of perspective drawing:

One Point Perspective – one vanishing point (VP), the object being viewed looking at the front or side.

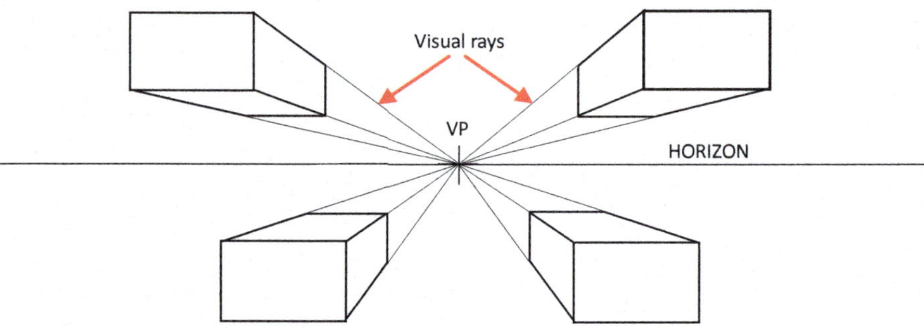

Two Point Perspective – two vanishing points (VP1, VP2), the object being viewed looking at a corner or edge.

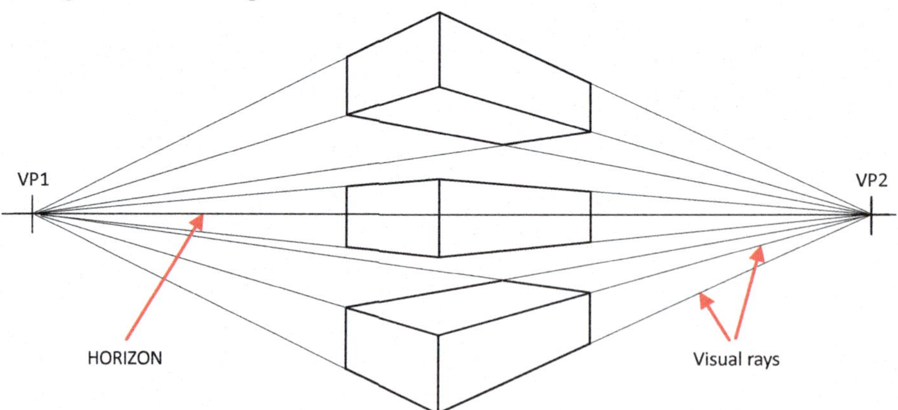

ISBN 978-0170185615

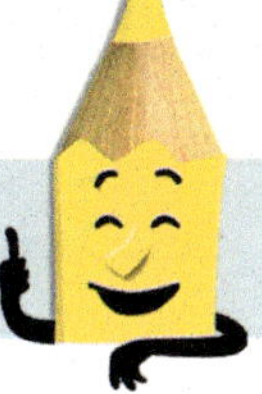

Use the following guidelines to help you complete **Worksheet 19 One Point Perspective**.

Exercise 1: Camera

One point perspective camera.

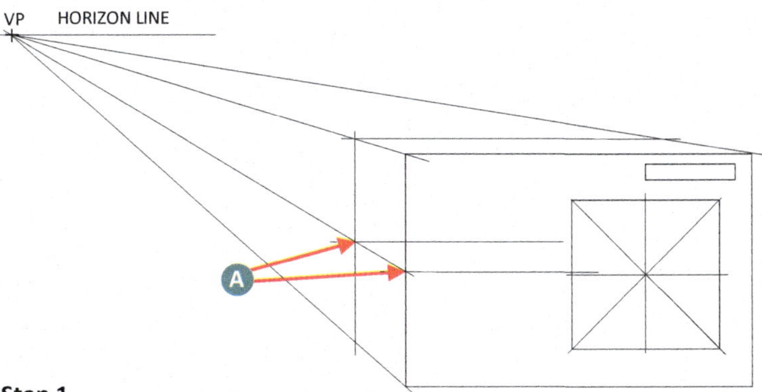

Step 1

Label the horizon line and the vanishing point.

From the starting points given, carefully draw the shape of the camera.

Draw the box that will become the lens (it will be square) and cross the diagonals to find the centre.

Find the middle of the back of the camera where the curved side will touch Ⓐ.

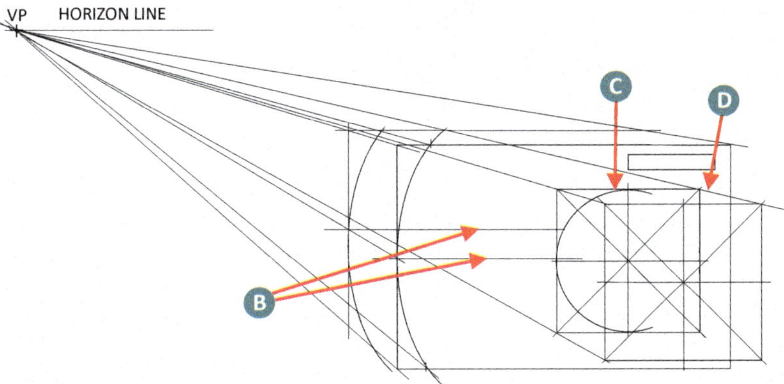

Step 2

Draw the curved ends. Step **R80** along lines Ⓑ from the end.

From the middle of the square,draw a part circle for the back of the lens Ⓒ.

Draw lines from the corners of the back square (Ⓓ) to the VP, then draw another square in front.

ISBN 978-0170185615

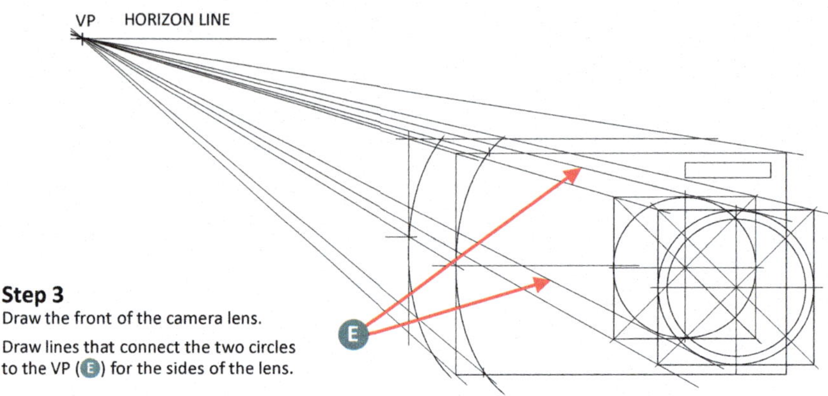

Step 3

Draw the front of the camera lens.

Draw lines that connect the two circles to the VP (E) for the sides of the lens.

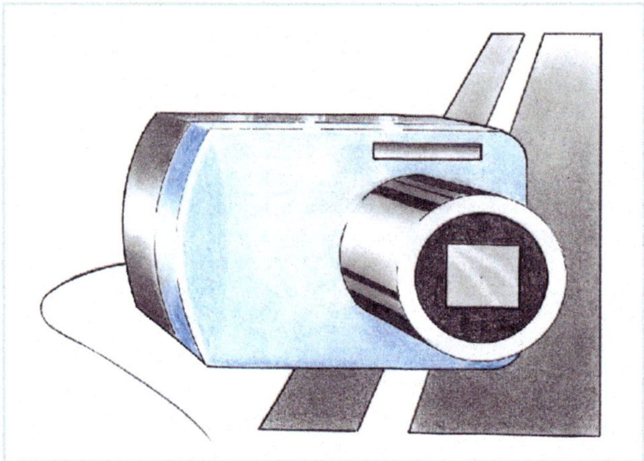

Finishing Your Drawing

4B pencil smudged with a tissue has been used for rendering the lens and the back half of the camera. (Note the extra line to separate the two halves of the camera body.) Vertical eraser stripes against an erasing shield make shine on top.

Colouring pencils have been used for the camera body. Note the white edges made with an eraser against an eraser shield.

The camera has been cut out and pasted onto a background of 4B pencil smudged with a tissue.

ISBN 978-0170185615

Exercise 2: Fence

Finding equal spaces when given the distance between each space.

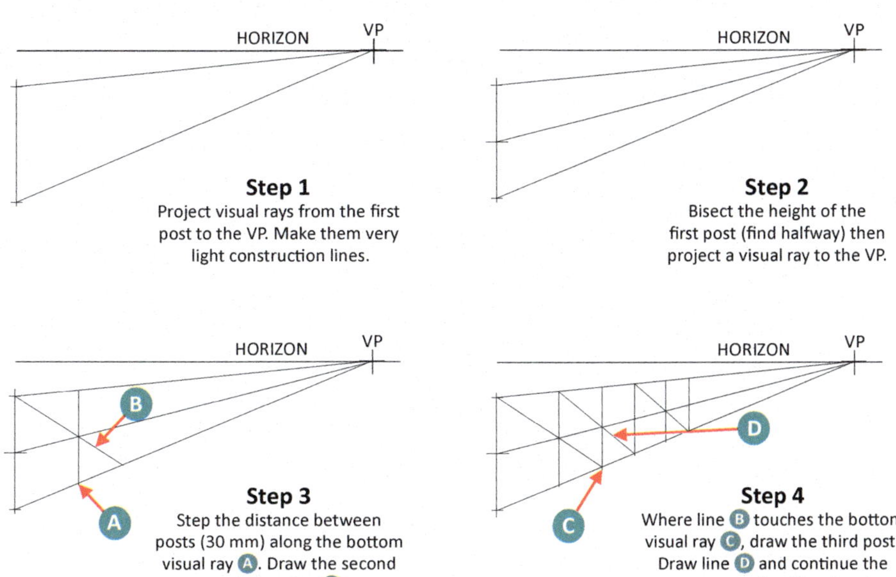

Step 1
Project visual rays from the first post to the VP. Make them very light construction lines.

Step 2
Bisect the height of the first post (find halfway) then project a visual ray to the VP.

Step 3
Step the distance between posts (30 mm) along the bottom visual ray A. Draw the second post then line B.

Step 4
Where line B touches the bottom visual ray C, draw the third post. Draw line D and continue the process for all posts.

Finishing Your Drawing

Colouring pencils have been used to render this drawing. All the techniques to do this have been used in your previous exercises. Remember the light direction for all drawings is from the left. Note the following:

- The top of each post is a narrow ellipse (oval shape). Draw these first. Make each post thinner as they get closer to the vanishing point.
- Shadows on the ground are horizontal.

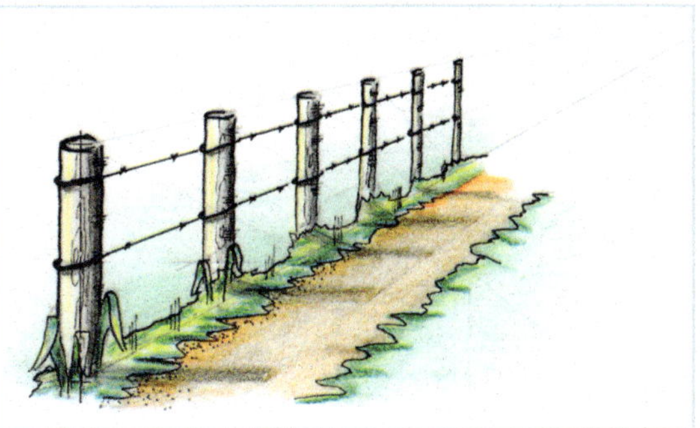

ISBN 978-0170185615

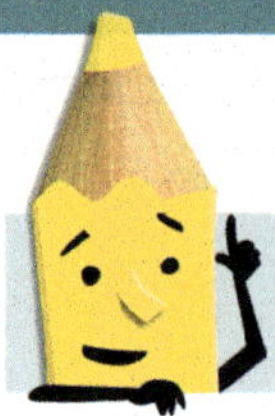

Use the following guidelines to help you complete **Worksheet 20 Two Point Perspective**.

Exercise 1: Kitchen Cupboard

Finding equal spaces.

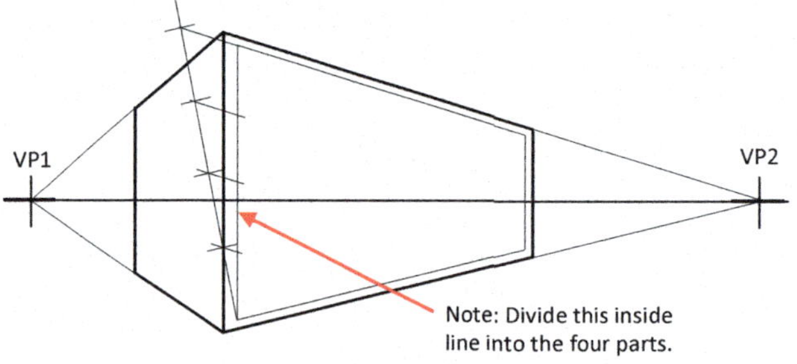

Step 1

Divide the height into the number of parts required (four). Use your compass as shown on page 56.

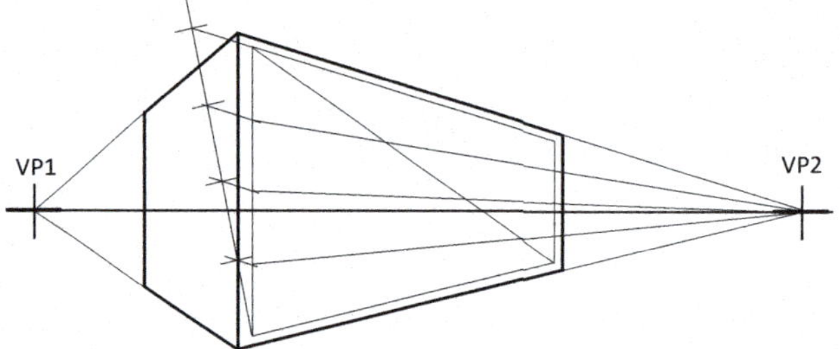

Step 2

Project visual rays to VP2 then cross the diagonal.

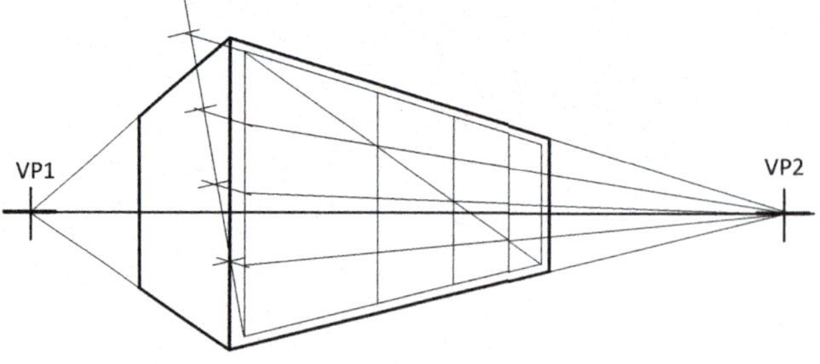

Step 3

Where the diagonal line meets the visual rays, draw vertical lines. You now have four spaces. They will appear to get closer together as they go towards VP2.

ISBN 978-0170185615

Exercise 2: Cottage

Finding centres and drawing the roof.

Step 1

- Draw the outline of the house by joining the dots given.
- Cross the diagonals of the end and draw a vertical line. This will locate the middle of the top of the roof.

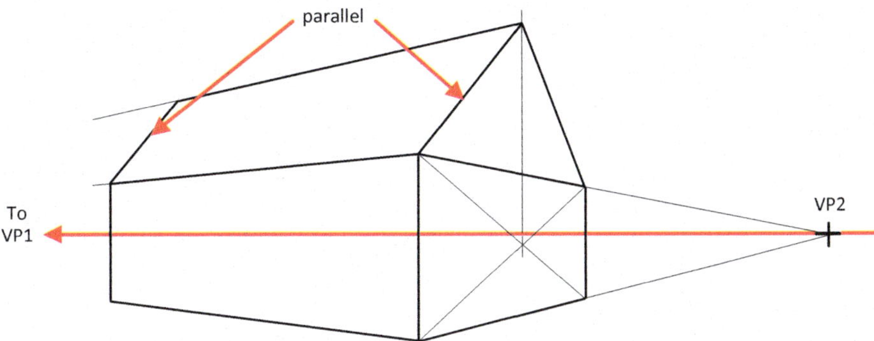

Step 2

- Extend line A 8 mm from the end of the roof.
- Draw lines B and C parallel to the angle of the roof (use your two set squares as shown on page 57).
- Draw a short vertical line D.

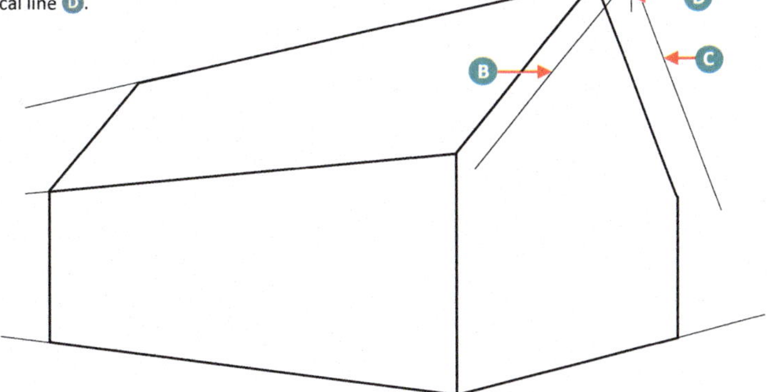

ISBN 978-0170185615

Step 3

- Draw the thickness of the end of the roof (E), parallel to line (B), up to line (D). Judge the distance from line (B). Then draw the opposite side from line (D), parallel to line (C).
- Measure 5 mm from (F) to (X). Draw a short line for the roof overhang, from VP1 through point **X**, up to point **Y**.
- Draw a line from VP2 through point **Y**. Continue it to meet line (E) and draw two short vertical lines to complete both ends of the roof.

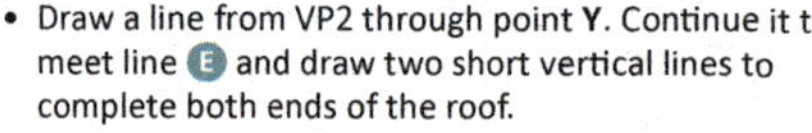

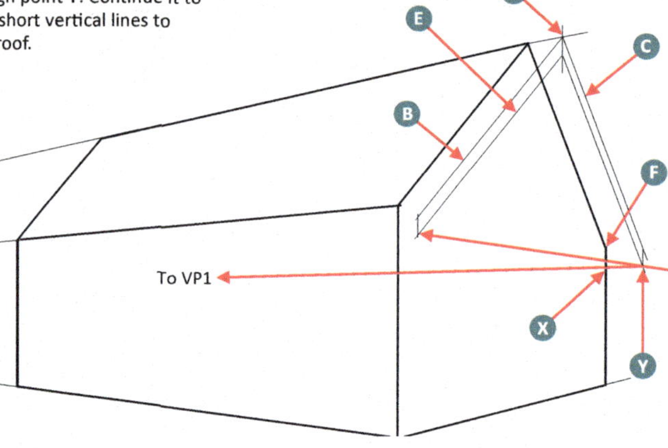

Step 4

- Extend lines to VP1 for the new side of the roof (Z).
- Continue the lines beyond the end of the house a short distance and draw the vertical line **V**.
- Draw the new end of the roof with a line parallel to the angle of the back of the roof.
- Erase the original roof line that is no longer needed.

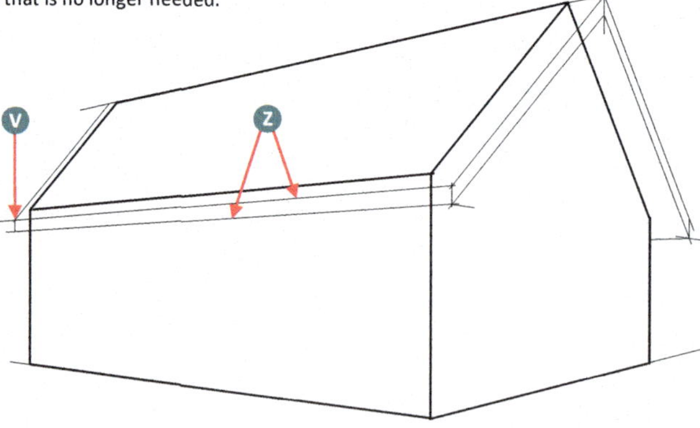

ISBN 978-0170185615

Finishing Your Drawings

Colouring pencils have been used to render this drawing. All the techniques to do this have been used in your previous exercises. Remember the light direction for all drawings is from the left. Note the following:

- Handles and hinges on the cupboard are drawn between visual rays to VP2.
- Windows on architectural drawings look best shaded black using reflections made with an eraser.
- Note the roof shadow on the walls.
- Architectural renderings should be lighter in the background and darker in the foreground.

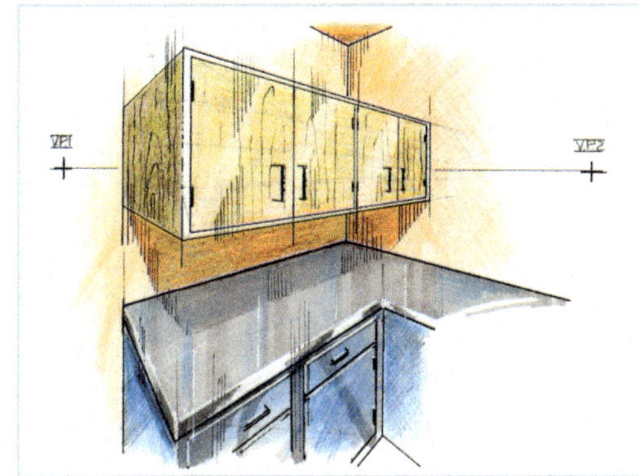

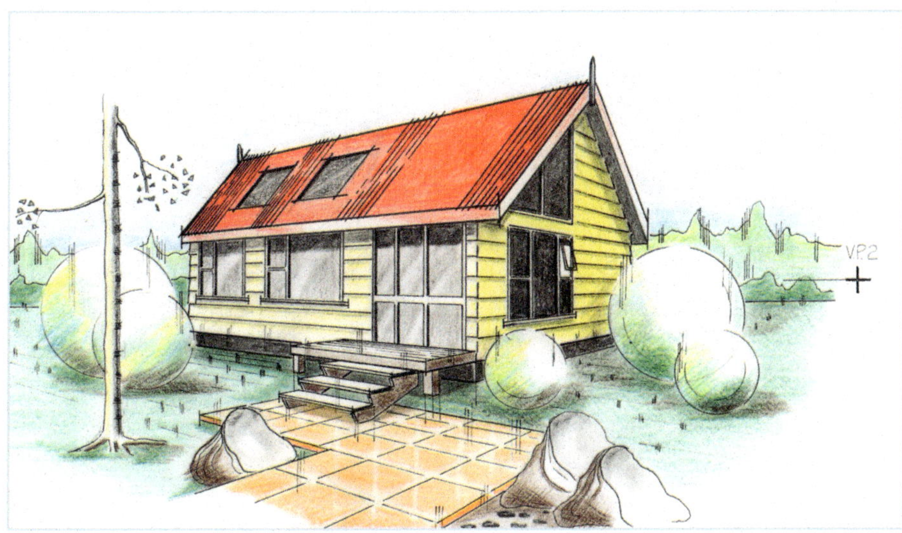

ISBN 978-0170185615

Regular Polygons: Method

Complete **Worksheet 22 Geometry – Polygons** using the methods below. Use a sharp 2H pencil, your compass and a straight edge. Outline the shape of each polygon leaving all constructions light but clearly seen.

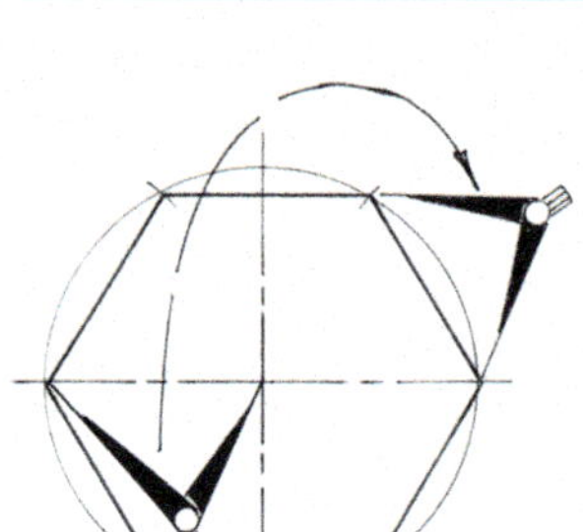

Hexagon constructed inside an ø80 circle.

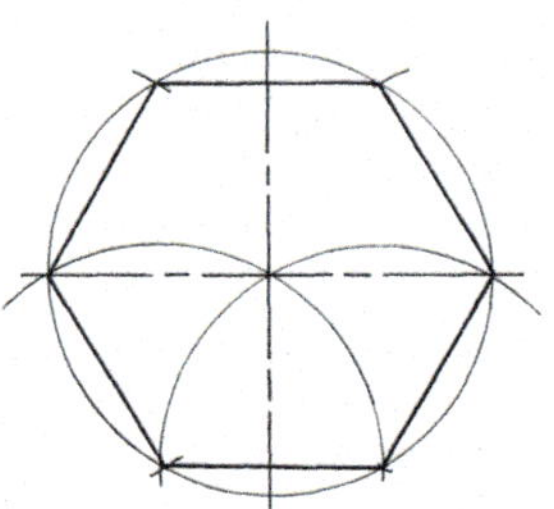

Hexagon constructed on a given line.

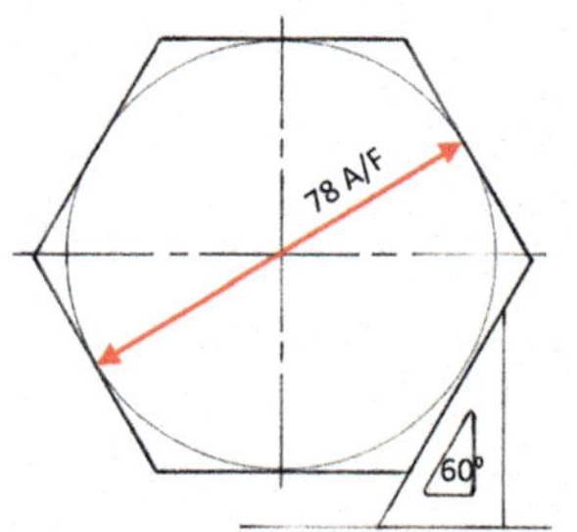

Hexagon constructed about a ø78 circle (78 A/F).
(A/F means Across the Flats.)

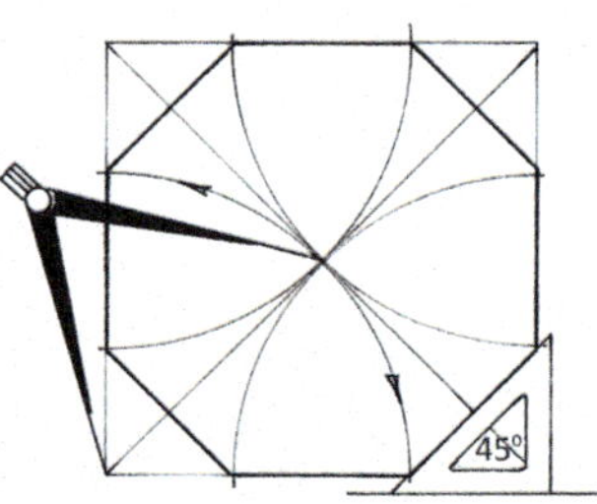

Octagon constructed inside an ø80 mm square.

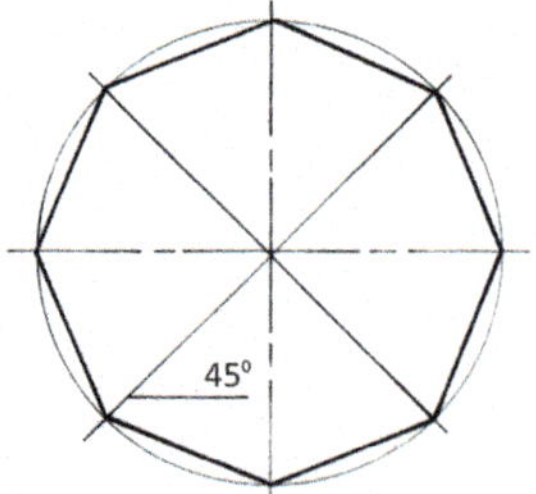

Octagon constructed inside an ø80 circle.

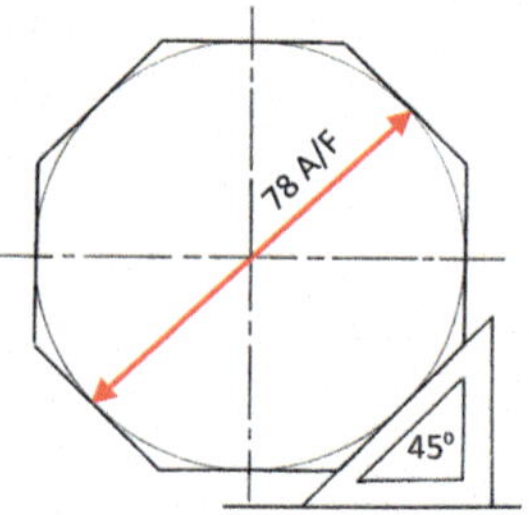

Octagon constructed about a ø78 circle (78 A/F).

ISBN 978-0170185615

Geometric Constructions: Method

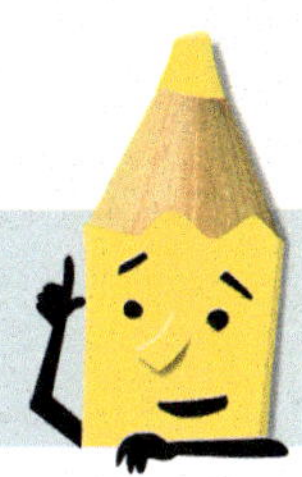

Complete **Worksheet 23 Geometry – Constructions** using the method below. Use a sharp 2H pencil, your compass and a straight edge. Leave all constructions light but clearly seen.

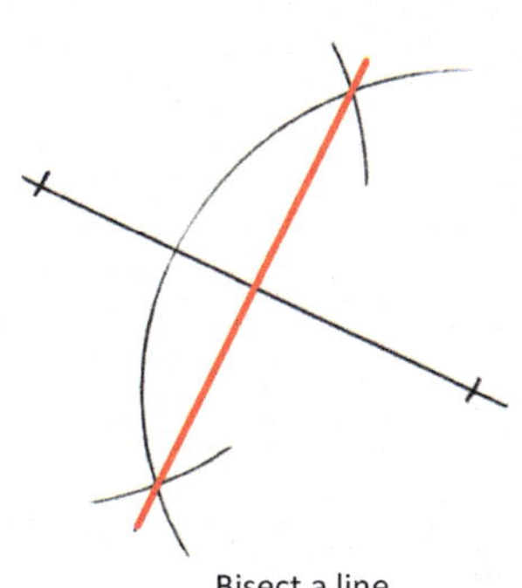

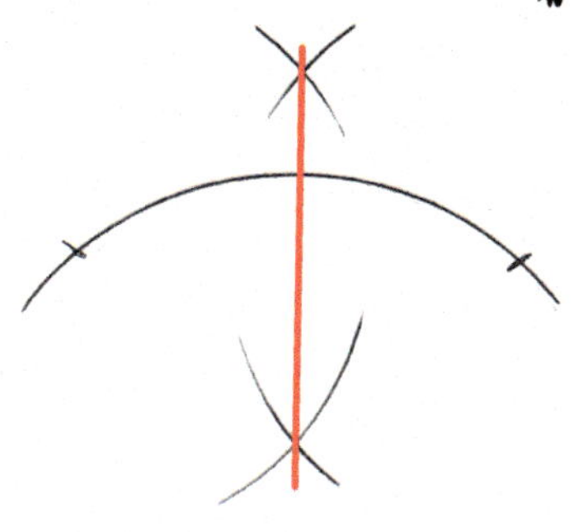

Bisect a line.

Bisect an arc.

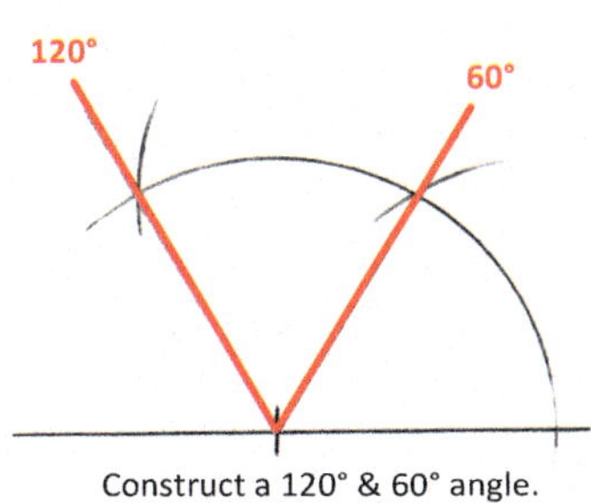

Construct a 120° & 60° angle.

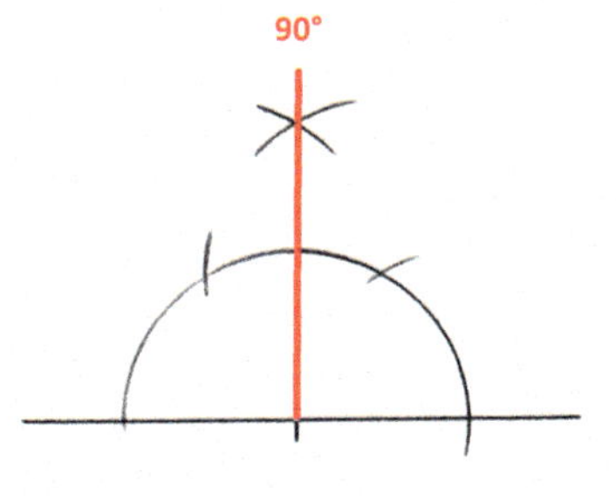

Construct a 90° angle (right angle).

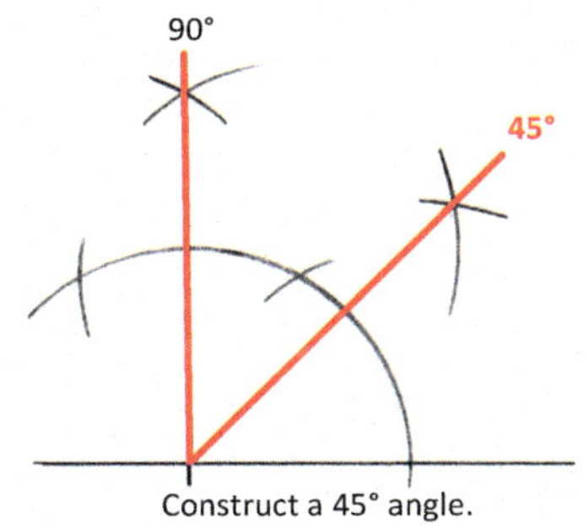

Construct a 45° angle.

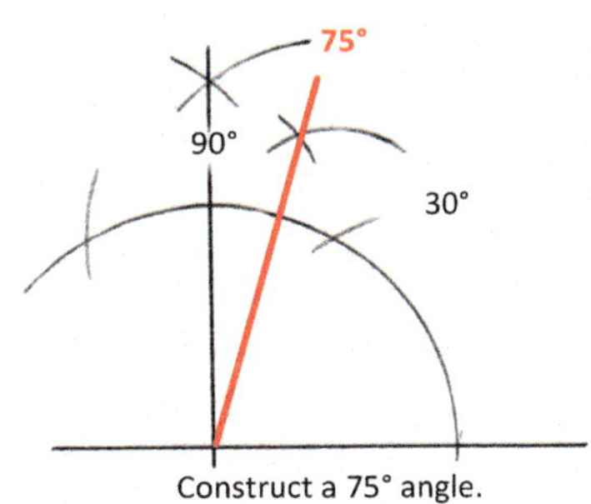

Construct a 75° angle.

ISBN 978-0170185615

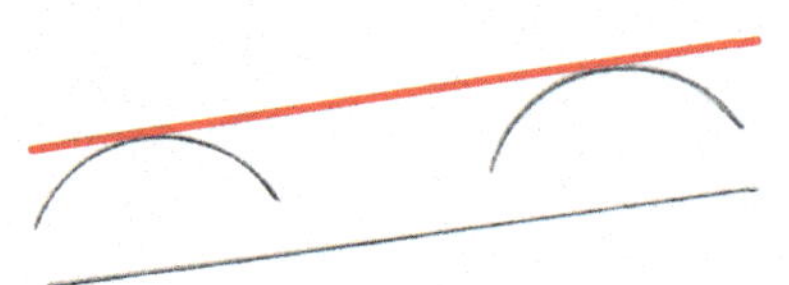

Draw a line parallel to another and 15 mm from it.

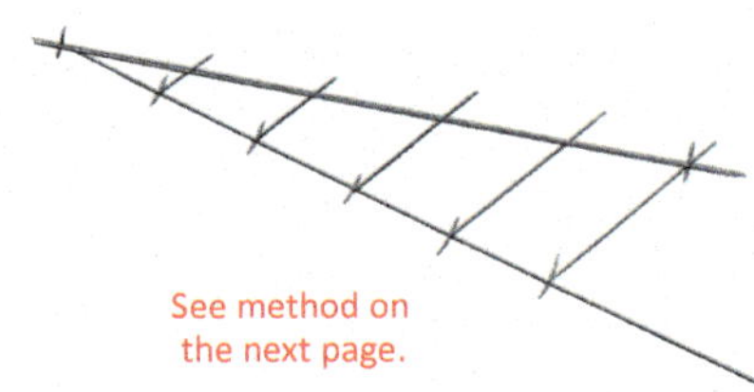

See method on the next page.

Divide a line into five equal parts.

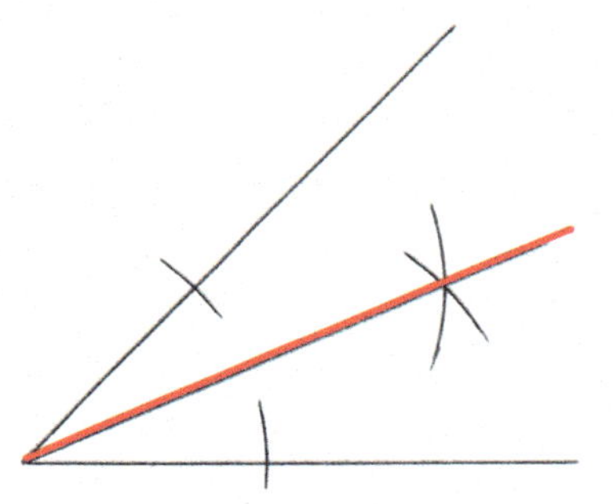

Bisect an angle.

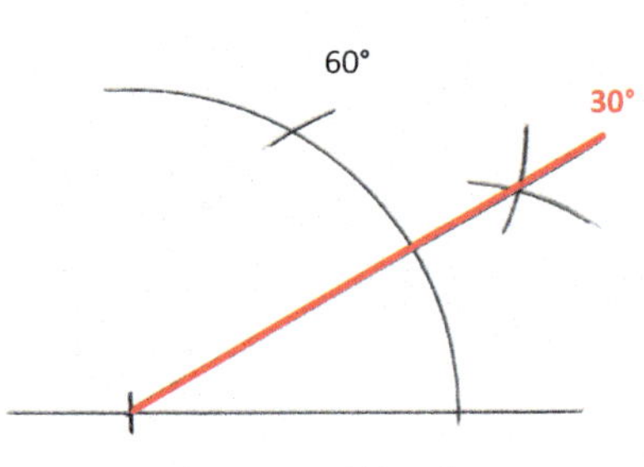

Construct a 30° angle.

Construct a square on a given base line.

ISBN 978-0170185615

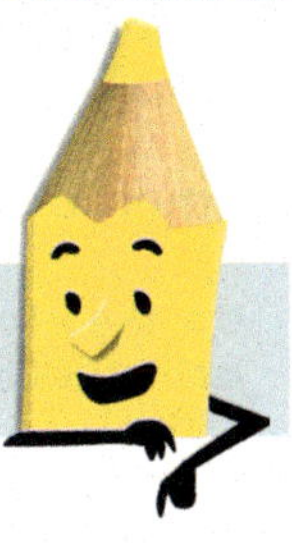

Dog Kennel – Dividing a Line into Equal Spaces

Use the following guidelines to help you complete **Worksheet 24 Angles in Isometric and Line Division.**

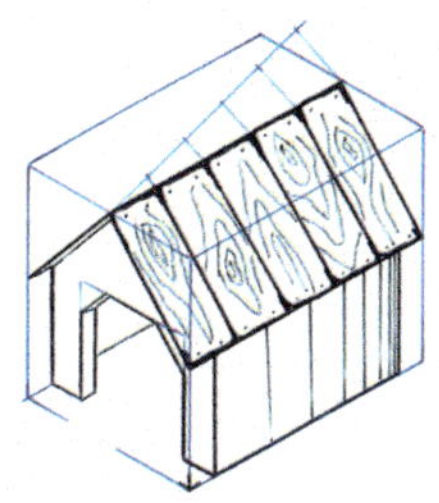

The steps below show how to divide a line of any length into a number of equal spaces without using a ruler.

In this case the spaces will form the five boards of the roof of a dog kennel.

The method can be used for any number of spaces and on a line that can be at any angle.

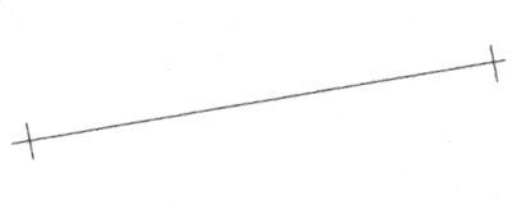

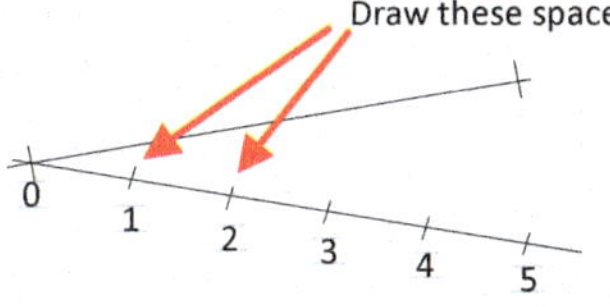

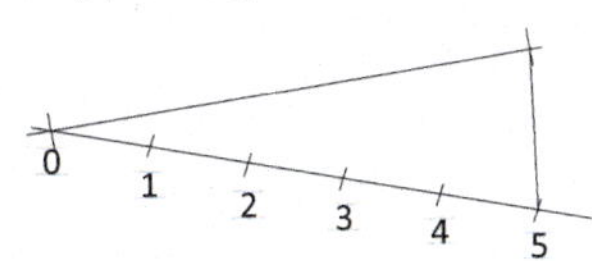

Step 1
Draw the line and set out the length you want to divide.

Step 2
Draw another line on any angle from any end. Set your compass to any distance and step out the number of spaces you want to divide the original line into.

Step 3
Join the last point (5) with a line to the end of the original line (this angle will vary depending on how big you make the spaces 1–5).

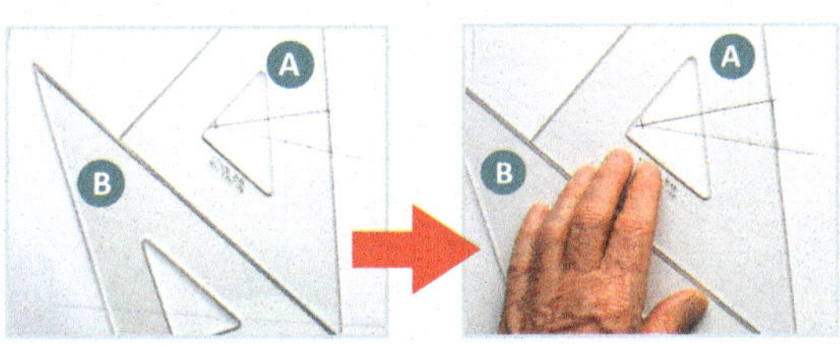

Step 4
Take both your set squares and line one edge (of A) up with the angle of the line at number 5.

Bring your other set square (B) to rest underneath.

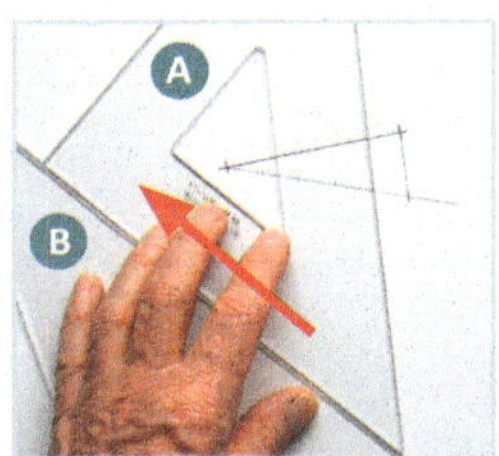

Step 5
While holding set square B, slide set square A along it to point 4. Draw a line up to the original line. Continue this process until all points have been drawn up to the original line. You now have your line divided into exactly five equal parts.

The process of sliding one set square along the edge of another allows you to make lines parallel to each other.

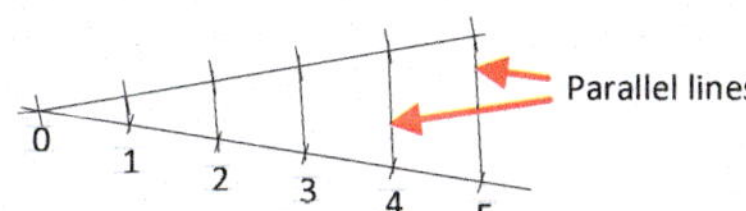

ISBN 978-0170185615

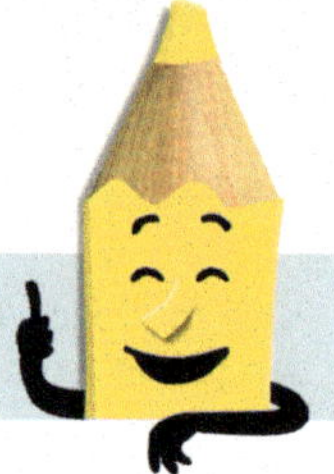

Isometric Chocolate Bar Box

Use the following guidelines to help you complete **Worksheet 25 Isometric Chocolate Bar Box.**

1 Prepare a new title block CHOCOLATE BAR BOX and use the layout shown.

2 Use the starting points given below to draw a front elevation and a left end elevation when viewed in the direction of the arrow. *Show clearly how you constructed the hexagonal end*. Judge sizes for the display window.

3 Using the end elevation as an auxiliary view, draw an isometric view of the box when the left end is towards you. *Show clearly all constructions. Use the starting point given below.*

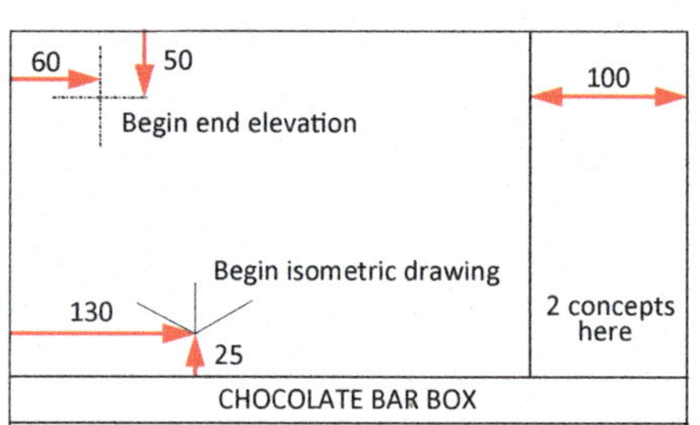

4 On the right side of the sheet, produce two concept sketches of your designs for graphics that could be placed on the outside of the box. Include a name for the box.

5 Indicate your chosen design, then place it onto the isometric drawing. Render the drawing to make it look real.

Box Dimensions
Overall length: 150 mm
Length of one edge of the hexagonal end: 25 mm

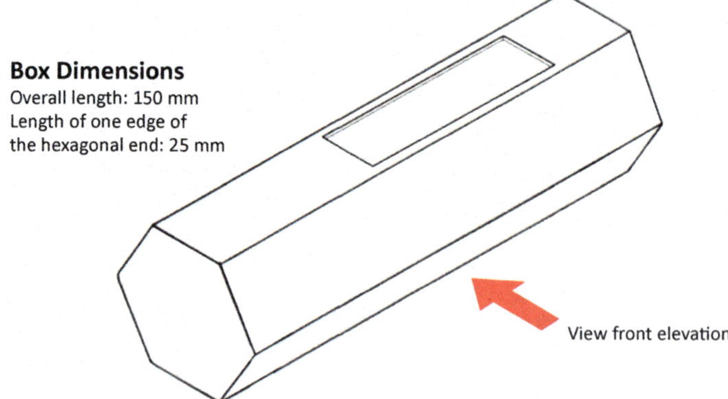

ISBN 978-0170185615

Isometric Chocolate Bar Box Method

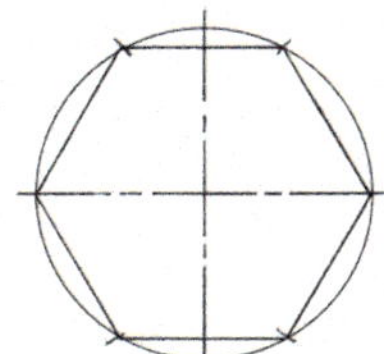

Step 1
Draw the regular hexagon end elevation. Make the lines medium darkness but not outlines.

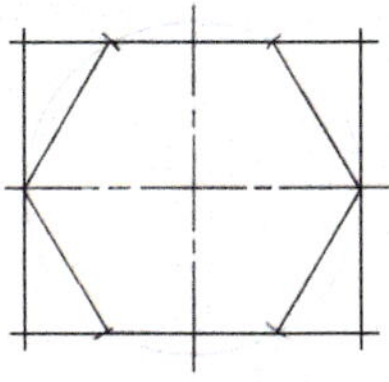

Step 2
Place a box around the hexagon. The drawing now becomes an auxiliary view (which means extra view). Label it as such.

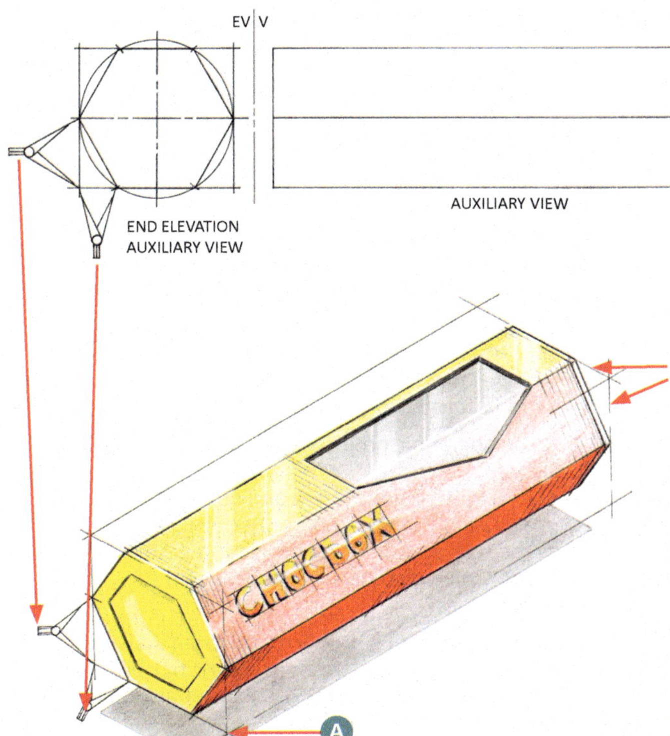

Step 3
Project the front elevation. Make the lines medium darkness but not outlines.

Step 4
Set out an isometric crate, the *same size as the orthographic views* to contain the shape of the box. Start at point A.

Use a sharp compass to transfer sizes from the auxiliary view. Make the lines construction lines.

Step 5
Inside the isometric crate, set out the shape of the hexagon.

Use a sharp compass to transfer sizes from the auxiliary view.

Place a display window on the top, check for accuracy, then outline the drawing. Leave construction lines clearly visible.

Step 6
Render and place your design on the drawing

ISBN 978-0170185615

Congratulations!

You now have all the skills you need to develop a set of drawings for your own design assignment. This section gives you the requirements of your brief and guidelines on how to present your solution.

Your brief is to be presented as a portfolio of work made up of your own A3 paper, approximately six sheets.

Refer back to the appropriate page of the textbook if you need to refresh your memory of certain skills.

Situation

You have just bought a new entertainment system but you have nowhere to store your CDs.

Design Brief

Design a unit to hold 10 CDs.

Design Specifications

The CD holder should:

- be free standing
- be robust
- be made from easy care materials
- hold 10 CDs
- be stylish.

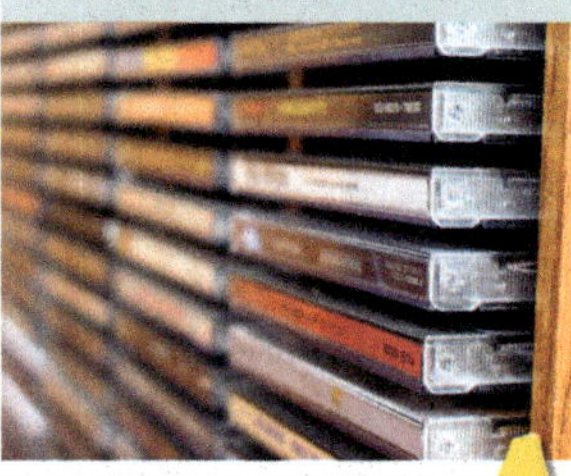

Don't forget to include your logo from **Worksheet 9 Logo Design**.

Requirements

1 Design Research and Concept Sketches
   - Cut and paste your research amongst your concepts.
   - Three concept sketches: one oblique, one isometric and one orthographic projection. *One A3 page.*

2 Design Development
   - Show a refinement of your concept ideas, details of how your design could be made (construction), final shape and the materials you think it could be made from. *One A3 page.*

3 Using design language, place brief notes about your research, concepts and design development sketches that relate to the specifications. Use the word *because*.

4 An orthographic projection, to scale, of your design. Show:
   - A plan, a front elevation and one end elevation, using correct projection.
   - The reference line and projection symbol.
   - The scale you have used printed in the title block.

5 Using instruments, produce a pictorial drawing of your final design (either isometric or oblique). Colour render this drawing, cut it out and paste it onto a background.

6 Produce a word processed final evaluation of your design. Use design language to discuss each specification.

ISBN 978-0170185615

Explanatory Notes

- This is a five week unit to be started at school and completed at home. It must be handed in complete on the due date.
- **Concept sketches** must use 2D and 3D freehand sketching methods. Show suitable lengths and widths, suitable shapes and styles, suitable materials etc.
- **Design development** sketches must use 2D and 3D freehand sketching methods. Where appropriate use exploded views. Show types of construction methods, types of finish, colour schemes.
- **3D freehand sketching methods** are isometric and oblique.
- **2D freehand sketching methods** are 3rd angle orthographic projection.
- **Design notes** must be used about research, concepts and design development sketches using the word 'because'. Your notes must use design language.
- **Design language** may be divided into two groups: Aesthetics and Function. Some examples of design language and their explanations are shown in the side bar:

AESTHETICS means:
The qualities of appearance, visual appeal, good taste and beauty. shape, colour, texture, finish, style, proportion, contrast, harmony
FUNCTION means:
How a product works or performs for its intended user. strength, durability, user friendliness, fitness for purpose

- Evaluation involves identifying the good features, faults, functions and aesthetics of your design. Use some design language to discuss how you incorporated the specifications into your design.

- **Texture** describes the look and feel of a surface.
- **Finish** describes the materials, paint or polish etc to be applied to a surface.
- **Proportion** describes sizes and shapes and their relationships to each other.
- **Style** is whether or not you think an object or shape is 'in fashion' or ugly or pleasing.
- **Harmony** describes different parts of a design that blend well together.
- **Contrast** describes opposing parts of a design such as clashing colours or shapes.
- **Durability** describes the ability of a product or material to stand up to wear.
- **Ergonomics** describes a design or parts of a design that are shaped to be used by the human form. *ie; computer game hand controller, tables and chairs etc.*
- **Fitness for purpose** describes how well a product works in the situation it was designed for.

ISBN 978-0170185615

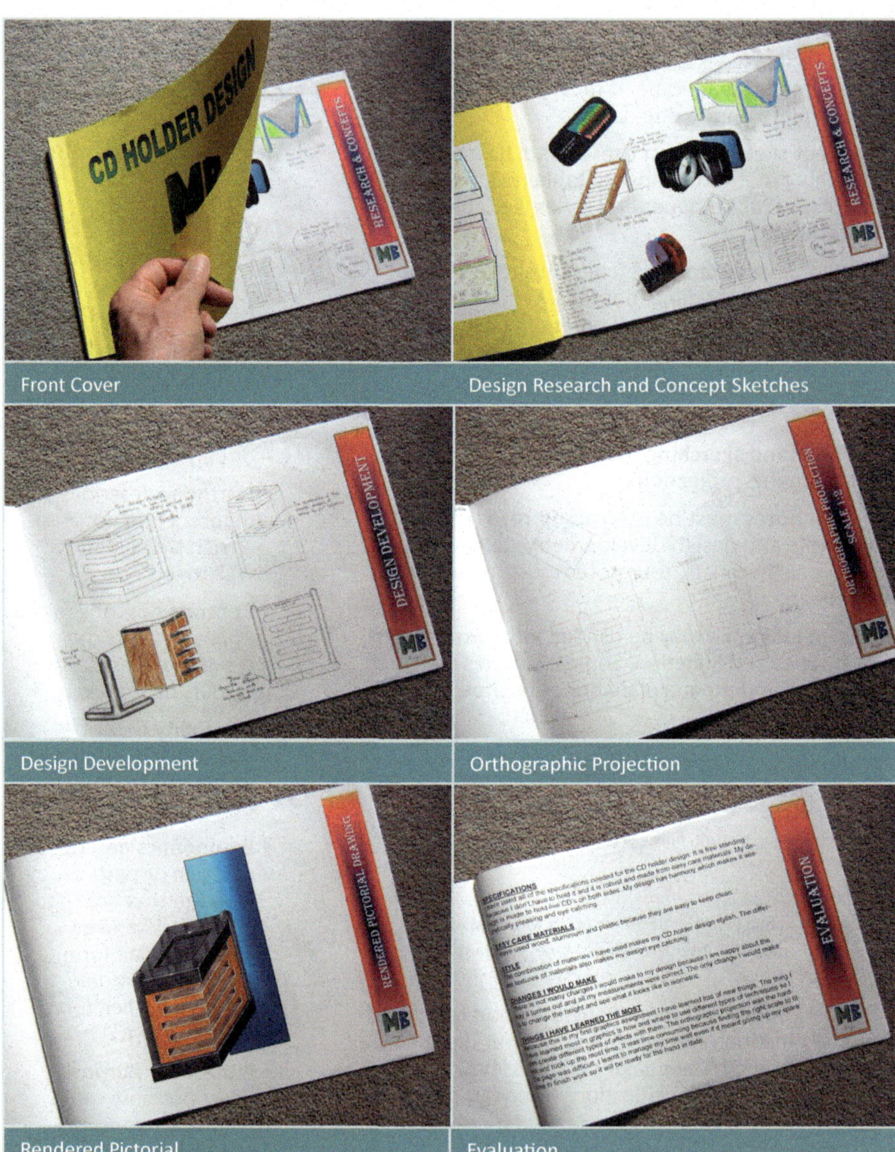

Front Cover

Design Research and Concept Sketches

Design Development

Orthographic Projection

Rendered Pictorial

Evaluation

ISBN 978-0170185615

This page shows a suggested assessment schedule based on the NCEA marking system. It may be modified to suit. Design assignments form the basis of NCEA Graphics.

<table>
<tr><th colspan="3">Year 9 GRAPHICS DESIGN ASSIGNMENT
ASSESSMENT SCHEDULE CD HOLDER DESIGN</th><th>NAME:</th></tr>
<tr><th>Evidence</th><th>Achievement</th><th>Achievement with MERIT</th><th>Achievement with EXCELLENCE</th></tr>
<tr><td rowspan="8">The Design Process Chart:
Completed and accurate.
Research:
Research of existing designs with notes.
Concepts:
Three concepts (2D, 3D), specifications addressed, design language, quality of sketching.
Design Development:
2D & 3D, specifications addressed, construction detail, design language, quality of sketching.
Orthographic Projection:
Accuracy, scale, standards, lines, layout.
Pictorial Drawing:
Instrumental constructions, skills, lines, standards.
Rendering:
Realism, use of media.
Title Blocks:
On all pages, accuracy.
Evaluation:
Specs addressed, clarity of script, design language.
Presentation:
All parts of the work are assembled with a front cover for assessment.</td><td>Some research is evident.</td><td>A range of research is evident with links to concepts.</td><td>A range of research is evident with links to concepts.</td></tr>
<tr><td>An attempt at concepts is made.</td><td>Two concepts are evident showing some links to research. Chosen concept is highlighted.</td><td>Three concepts (2D and 3D) are shown with links to research. Chosen concept highlighted.</td></tr>
<tr><td>Some design development is attempted.</td><td>Good development showing some construction detail.</td><td>2D and 3D development sketches are detailed and complex.</td></tr>
<tr><td>Design notes are evident.</td><td>Design notes are evident with some design language used.</td><td>Design notes relate to specs with justification for decisions using design language.</td></tr>
<tr><td>An orthographic projection is attempted.</td><td>An orthographic projection is drawn to scale with good overall skills, understanding and line quality evident.</td><td>A high quality orthographic projection is drawn to scale with excellent skills, understanding and line quality evident.</td></tr>
<tr><td>A pictorial drawing is attempted with some rendering evident.</td><td>A good pictorial drawing is produced showing sound rendering skills.</td><td>A high quality pictorial drawing, demonstrating excellent media use with resulting realism.</td></tr>
<tr><td>An evaluation is attempted.</td><td>Evaluation addresses some specifications with some design language used.</td><td>Full evaluation addresses all the specifications with fluent use of design language.</td></tr>
<tr><td>Some work is assembled.</td><td>Good quality work is assembled and presented.</td><td>High quality work is assembled and well-presented.</td></tr>
<tr><td colspan="2">NA = Not Achieved   A = Achieved
M = Merit   E = Excellence</td><td colspan="2">Overall Level of Performance</td></tr>
</table>

ISBN 978-0170185615

Worksheet Mark Schedules Explanation

The mark schedules are given to provide teacher feedback to the student, based on the NCEA system of marking which begins at Level 1 in Year 11.

They are not intended to be read in conjunction with any explanatory notes; rather they are provided to introduce students to the terminology of Not Achieved, Achieved, Merit and Excellence.

As a general rule, the following grade boundaries should apply:

Not Achieved = requires attention / incomplete
Achieved = acceptable work
Merit = good work
Excellence = high quality work

An example of a completed schedule and the overall Level of Performance is shown at right.

Marks	N	A	M	E
Lines (weight/precision)		X		
Title block			X	
Printing standard				X
Overall accuracy			X	
Overall level of performance				A
N=Not Achieved A=Achieved M=Merit E=Excellence				

Teachers should feel free to use other marking systems if preferred. Whatever system is used, it is important that students receive feedback and that the marks are a fair reflection of the quality and understanding of their work.

Work should be returned to students promptly after marking.

Examples of good work should be displayed in the classroom.

ISBN 978-0170185615